SHORT STACK PUBLISHING

# HOW TO HANDLE YOUR RECRUITMENT CONSULTANT

Herbie Henderson lives in London with her delectable husband and her genius dog Harry. With a head packed full of insider knowledge (thanks to her experience as a recruitment consultant) Herbie set about creating this How to Handle. She knew just how slippery and sloppy some of her competitors could be, and how notoriously difficult they were to handle. She also knew that a lot of candidates out there had reached breaking or boiling point with their consultants. So she got to work interrogating competitors, colleagues, candidates and frankly anyone & everyone relevant; toiling tirelessly to unearth the best kept secrets (and some of the lousy consultants' regrettably unsavoury practices) so you now you can discover... **How to Handle Your Recruitment Consultant** with phenomenal results.

Herbie would like to state for the record that all the agencies she has ever worked with have impeccable working practices, professional & perfect consultants, brilliant & brainy candidates and delicious & adorable clients.

SHORT STACK PUBLISHING
PRESENTS

# How to Handle Your Recruitment Consultant

Herbie Henderson

SHORT STACK PUBLISHING

This edition published in Great Britain by Short Stack Publishing

www.shortstackpublishing.com

10 9 8 7 6 5 4 3 2

#5 in The How to Handle Series
Series Editor Oscar Dyson

ISBN-13: 978-1-906467-05-0

# CONTENTS

# A HEADS UP ON ABBREVIATIONS, PHRASEOLOGY & ASSUMPTIONS *BEFORE* YOU START READING

**RCs:** Rather than waste your reading time, the rainforests' trees and the printer's ink I'll mostly abbreviate the term 'Recruitment Consultant' to 'RC'. (Apologies to those of readers who dislike the term 'Recruitment Consultant' and feel it's a jumped up title for a very ordinary job - but come on... it's widely accepted, I didn't come up with it, and let's not get our collective knickers in a twist obsessing over a job title.)

**Talking of collective:** There are probably several of you who have many suggestions for an appropriate collective noun for RCs working together (The more tame ones I've heard include 'An Annoyance of Recruitment Consultants', 'A Bother of Recruitment Consultants' and 'A Buffoonery of Recruitment Consultants'... I'll leave the less palatable ones to your imagination). However, for the avoidance of doubt, in organisational terms people tend to refer to a group of RCs working together as a Recruitment Consultancy or as an Agency. (I know of one RC who doesn't like the word 'agency' for some reason (though I suspect he'd prefer it to buffoonery)). Anyway, to cut to the chase, 'agency' is the term I'll be using...

**You:** I'm making a basic assumption that you're a decent candidate. In fact I'm assuming you're better than decent, you're savvy and you're smart because you've sussed the need to handle your RCs and that's why this book is in your hands, and you're not just leaving it to chance. Don't get me wrong, I'm not assuming you're a Nobel Prize winning Mensan with a double first from Oxford who rescues small animals and children in your spare time, (when you're not putting the finishing touches to your economic program that'll rid the world of all poverty). I'm just assuming you're a bright, personable, capable candidate who's smart enough to know that if you need to brush up on some skills to improve your value in the marketplace then you'll get on and do that without needing me to tell you what to do... that, after all, is *not* what this book is all about.

**And finally:** With the best will in the world I cannot *promise* you'll get the job you want, because whilst the buck ultimately stops with you, there are also a host of variables that I couldn't control on your behalf unless I was God (or whatever omnipotent, omniscient, omnipresent being may be responsible for the variables in your job search). In fact if I had made such a foolish and empty promise I'd hope you'd have flung this book back on the shelf, because you're a smart cookie and you'd know I was talking out of my... (it rhymes with farce). I can however provide you with all the tools, techniques and advice possible for you to then apply and implement, thus making sure your RC maximises their performance, which will boost you into the position where you *can* land the job of your dreams!

So it's RCs and agencies, you're a pretty damned good candidate (though you're not superhuman) and between us you and I are going to kick your RCs into shape.

**Phew. Right. Now that's all cleared up let's get on with it.**

## Chapter One

# THE BEGINNING
# A VERY GOOD PLACE TO START
### (AND DON'T IGNORE THE SERIOUS WARNING!)

So you've seen an agency advert for your ideal job,
you know you're the *ideal* candidate, the smartest,
the best qualified, you have just the right experience,
you're the perfect match, have a CV to die for, you give
great interview, the office is just 10 minutes from your flat
and you don't mind working for peanuts?

And yet those useless, arrogant, smug, ignorant, lazy SOBs
at the agency *still* haven't got back to you?

Let's make them get their act together so you can land your ideal job.

### INTRODUCTION

**Why are you reading this?**
Chances are that you're here because you're currently looking for a job, and you're totally and utterly fed up of useless Recruitment Consultants not living up to their promises or to your expectations.

**Why have I written this?**
I'll admit it: I was a Recruitment Consultant. I also admit I really enjoyed it (so much so that I still keep my hand in...). And I know from first hand experience that whilst there are some totally cracking RCs, sadly there are some completely lousy ones out there too. I want to help you differentiate between them; which isn't always as easy as it may seem (they can be conniving little devils). I want to help you unearth the good ones, avoid the lousy ones, spot the disingenuous and unscrupulous ones and manage the mediocre ones. They all need handling in some shape or form (even the good ones). And frustratingly you'll find it's not just the good ones who have the juicy jobs you want. You need to know how to handle them *all*.

## The Unique Selling Point of this How to Handle?

The USP of this book is that it's wholly focussed on helping you get the very best possible performance out of your RCs. We're going to blow the lid of the underhand practices, the sloppy systems and the cruddy communication to put you back in the driving seat where you should be.

I know first hand how exhilarating it can be when you have a great (and mutually beneficial) relationship between candidate and RC, and I know how skin crawlingly, teeth gratingly infuriating it is when the relationship just doesn't work. I want you to experience the former.

There's a wealth of great books *for* RCs telling them how to be amazing recruitment consultants (even the most cursory of general internet or Amazon searches reveals that). But, unfortunately, as far as I can tell it seems that an awful lot of the consultants who should have read them, haven't. (And that alone is a good reason for you to read *this* book.) Fact is; this is the only book that teaches *you*, the candidate, how to handle those slippery little suckers.

## So is this Poacher turned Gamekeeper Territory?

Short answer: No.

Longer answer: Not exactly. I'm not turning against the very people I used to work with in recruitment. I have the greatest respect for the good RCs, although admittedly I do reserve a particular loathing for the lousy, lazy RCs who let the side down and give the rest of us a bad name. Whether you've picked up this book because you've reached the end of your tether with your existing or past RCs, or whether you're just venturing into the marketplace for the first time, chances are you've heard horror stories about RCs, but please believe me: we're NOT all like that.

Anyway, that point aside for one minute, having worked within the industry I think I'm well positioned to be able to say that in my humble opinion, from time to time all RCs need handling to greater or lesser degrees.

## How have I discovered how to get the most out of RCs?

Honestly? I've looked, listened and learned. I've seen RCs handled brilliantly and I've seen them handled badly, and seen the delicious and disastrous (respectively) outcomes of both. I've quizzed and badgered industry experts, colleagues, competitors, clients, applicants and of course candidates. Then I've thrown it all into the blender in my head, combined it with my personal insider knowledge and experiences, and come up with this book. You're going to have a unique insight into what goes on in the little (sometimes very very little) grey cells of *your* RCs. But, most pertinently, you're going to know how to use that information and more, meaning you can handle those RCs so masterfully that you'll get the absolute best out of them in everything they do (and best of all, they won't even realise they're being handled).

## How to make the most of this book:

Handling an RC intelligently isn't rocket science (obviously). And anyway... it's more of an art than a science... an astonishingly under practiced art at that, and one that results in job opportunities being missed. Of course, now, that fact is going to work in your favour. Your competitors in the marketplace (candidates going for the same jobs as you) will mishandle their RCs, they'll be unprepared for them and they'll miss the opportunities that you'll be enjoying and revelling in. They'll be waiting crossly for their calls to be returned whilst you're merrily cherry picking your interviews, and later on job offers.

By reading this and putting the techniques into practice, your RCs are going to be like putty in your hands. You'll be in the strongest position possible, thanks to understanding the process from the inside out. You're going to be privy to insider tips, tricks, strategies and secrets that'll differentiate you from your contemporaries and crucially put you one step ahead not only of your RCs but also of your competitors in the marketplace.

Successful handling of your RCs will result in them being inspired by you, excited by the prospect of placing you, and make them grab the phone when you call (and rush to return any missed calls from you). You'll have them busting their buns, moving heaven and earth to get you the best possible job (and package) with all the trimmings.

So settle in, take heed and scribble copious notes in the margins, in fact in any white space at all, and go wild with your highlighter pens (unless this is a library copy, in which case it's probably best that you don't...). Read it cover to cover on your morning commute, or dip in and out of it as you sit on the loo, it's entirely your call.

## ☠    A SERIOUS WARNING    ☠

Let's deal with an uncomfortable reality (I would have said an inconvenient truth... but that phrase has been hijacked rather). In fact the sooner we get it out of the way the better. Throughout this book at various points we'll be dealing with issues that only arise because there are some RCs who are just plain lousy. This lousiness manifests itself in many forms, the RC in question may be: lazy, ineffectual, inefficient, forgetful, deceitful, sloppy, unprofessional, unscrupulous, arrogant, ignorant, illiterate, cocky, pushy, apathetic, aggressive, generally unpleasant or downright rude. Now of course not all of these 'evils' are equal or indeed always bad... after all *pushiness* when it's on your side as they strong arm a client into meeting with you, can be a good thing, a very very good thing. Nevertheless the unpalatable truth is that the lousy RCs exist, and there's no getting away from it. But remember those RCs are the exception and not the norm.

I realise that the more world-weary readers (possibly those who have already had bad experiences with one or more RCs) may be tempted to treat all RCs with suspicion ...with disdain. Don't. Really don't.

Big growly dogs smell fear *(...allegedly).*
*(That is your pant wetting fear of them as big growly dogs)*
This makes some big growly dogs bite you *(...allegedly).*
*(That is their teeth in your butt...)*

Recruitment consultants smell disdain *(...unquestionably).*
*(That is your lip-curling disdain for them as RCs)*
This makes some of them dislike you and decide not to make any effort at all under any circumstances to place you
*(...unquestionably).*
*(That is, under no circumstances whatsoever... none... zip.. nemmeno uno... not even if the devil took up ice skating...)*

In a nutshell most people in recruitment take quite a lot of flak, are the butt of almost as many jokes as estate agents and are often treated like a boil on the butt of mankind. So reign in your disdain, and afford them the common courtesy of an open mind.
Trust me, you'll be doing yourself a big favour.

OK. So, at this point you may well be thinking "Cuh. Yeah. Whatever. It's not as though I have to use RCs anyway." (Or words to that effect.) Good point. So let's very quickly run through the alternatives and why RCs really can be your greatest asset.

## YOUR BASIC OPTIONS

Obviously, as the book title states, this publication is all about handling your RCs. However I'm not suggesting for a moment that RCs are your only option. Although I do think that thanks to bad handling they are an under utilised option; by which I mean candidates may register but they don't get the most out of their RCs by a long chalk. So, just briefly, apart from the RC option what are your alternative routes to market?

### Your Possible Routes to Market:

Broadly speaking you have five.

**1) Approach Recruitment Consultants directly:**
- Responding to an advertised vacancy (in print or online)
- Speculatively (not responding to a specific advertisement)

**2) Approach Organisations (Potential Employers) Directly:**
- Responding to an advertised vacancy (print or online)
- Approach speculatively

**3) Register your CV on one or more internet jobsites:**
- This will hopefully result in either a potential employer or (the more likely of the two) an agency contacting you directly to discuss opportunities.

**4) Through Personal Contacts / Networking:**
- Hearing on the grapevine of forthcoming vacancies and/or utilising personal contacts to get a foot in the door.

**5) Getting head hunted or poached...** lucky, lucky you!

As stated above, this book obviously focuses on the first route.

## RCs: THE BENEFITS

If you're reading this, you've most probably already decided to use (or at the very least you're considering using) RCs. But even so you may not have deliberately given thought to the benefits of doing so. I'm going to run through them here, because once you have them fixed in your head it may just help you maintain focus when the whole process is driving you nuts! And, of course, it helps you remember why it really *is* worth handling them.

## So, Why Use Recruitment Consultants?

A really good RC is, in essence, like a fabulous matchmaker with an enviable little black book. And, without wishing to strangle the metaphor to death, doesn't that have its appeal when compared to just responding randomly to a lonely hearts advert along with a gazillion other singletons gagging for a date?

On a more practical and business-like note, a good RC is not in the business of selling jobs or people, they're in the business of identifying good market matches and if anything, are selling information and knowledge. They know of jobs that are available and they know of candidates that are available; the skill is all in the mixing and matching.

So, for you as a candidate what does this mean in terms of opportunities? In essence, a good RC will:

**1) Expand your opportunities:** A good RC will introduce you to a far wider range of job opportunities than you could ever unearth by yourself, not because you aren't a determined grafter, but simply because RCs have access to information and people that you don't.

**2) Utilise their contacts and their database:** They'll get you into interviews with organisations you're interested in and which would be right for you. These may be organisations with whom they already have strong relationships (which is great for you), or there may be organisations they'll approach on your behalf and their recommendation of you will carry weight simply because of who they are. Believe it or not RCs and agencies with good reputations are respected and their opinions are valued by clients.

**3) Refine your search:** A good RC will help you to refine your search; identifying opportunities that would be right for you, and prevent you going on wild goose chases and chasing down blind alleys. They'll help prevent you wasting effort and valuable time.

**4) Provide access to insider knowledge:** They'll be able to give you the inside track on new jobs just in, or forthcoming opportunities that are not yet public knowledge. Don't forget that often RCs know about forthcoming openings before employers. How and why? Because many of the very individuals who come a register to search for new jobs, have not yet handed in their notice to their existing employers, and RCs know they'll need replacing.

**5) Provide even MORE insider knowledge so you have the inside track and the edge over competitors at interview:** When you're invited to interview with prospective employers RCs will give you the low down on the organisation, the people, the team etc. They'll work with you to ensure you're properly and thoroughly briefed before all your job interviews. Thus you'll know all you can about the company, its culture, the teams and the dynamics relevant to the opportunities you're pursuing (and not just the comparatively tame and mundane information that the prospective employer will have listed on their website).

**6) Be your only option...** And last but not least, and I know some candidates resent it, a lot of organisations simply will not accept direct applications. Such organisations elect to work only with well respected agencies, thus outsourcing the early stages of their recruitment process.

The five main reasons for this are:

**a) SPEED:** It's quicker for the organisations in many cases. RCs may well have the perfect candidate (is that you?) sitting on their books; ready, waiting and raring to go.

**b) AGGRO:** It's less aggravation. Organisations often want to outsource the early headachy stages of the process (the adverts, the initial screening of CVs and letters, the phone calls, the rejections, the first interviews, the organising of the later interviews).

**c) DISCRETION:** The profile of the organisation or individual  employer is such that they don't want the recruitment process to draw any attention. They want to be as discreet as possible so no obvious adverts etc.

**d) COST:** Recruiting is expensive for an organisation, (without even including 'big picture' costs of training etc). If they do it themselves, they either have full time members of staff devoted to it, or they have to pull someone away from their 'proper job' to focus on the recruiting process. This is in part why some organisations would rather pay a fee to an agency for finding them a new recruit/new recruits.

**e) THEY'VE FAILED IN THE PAST:** They've tried recruiting directly in the past and put bluntly they've been unable to attract the right calibre of candidate.

## A FEW FACTS & FIGURES
## SO YOU KNOW WHERE YOU STAND

To put into perspective how popular the RC route actually is, recent surveys[1] estimate that 83% to 87% of companies use RCs to fill their positions. Indeed the trend is for organisations to increasingly work with agencies, outsourcing their recruitment processes, in part if not entirely. And, purely as a matter of interest, these same surveys estimate that 89% of candidates use RCs in their job searches.

The recruitment industry is huge, and it's growing. According to The Recruitment & Employment Confederation[2], in the UK alone the industry is responsible for over 700,000 employees being placed in permanent work each year, and approximately 1.2 million temporary workers being out on assignment in any given week. Approximately 100,000 people in the UK work in recruitment... and it's an industry that's worth £24.5 billion.

HEY! YOU?! WAKE UP! Don't tune out and start snoozing because there was less than half a page of stats! I know all that seemed boring; I simply want to put into perspective just what a big industry recruitment is, and why to be honest it's so important you know how to handle the people who work within it to your advantage. But did you see how quickly you lost interest then? Didn't take long did it? Remember that when constructing covering letters and CVs! But, back to the point, RCs are a fact of job hunting life, so let's get on and make the most of them.

[1] Chartered Institute of Personnel and Development (CIPD), Recruitment, Retention and Turnover 2004, Gordon Yates/Guardian Annual Survey 2002

[2] http://www.rec.uk.com/

# Chapter Two

# THE NOTEBOOK OF SUCCESS
# A SIMPLE SECRET

*"Everyone has a photographic memory.*
*Some don't have film."*

You may have been (hoping?) expecting me to reveal a big RC secret about RCs' notebooks. Sorry to disappoint, but I'm not (not yet anyway). Although I'll admit, I do know of RCs who keep, or have kept, secret notebooks with 'off the record' remarks about their clients and candidates. (As it happens the comments aren't half as bad as you may imagine, they're mostly pretty innocent notes that help RCs remember who you are, what you are looking for etc, then some comment or other that means something to them but wouldn't be appropriate to be entered on formal records. This may be as innocent as 'Knew my sister at school' or may be the slightly less innocent 'Rates himself somewhat higher than I do. Smug & bit of a big head. Would fit in well at <insert organisation name eg: Cholmondeley Smythebottom's Private Bank>.) Now let's get back to the subject in hand: The Notebook of Success.

One of the fundamental tenets of successful job hunting is good organisation. Indeed a pretty standard recommendation in the oodles of job hunting books on the market is that you should keep a 'job file'. I'm not belittling this suggestion, in fact I wholeheartedly recommend it. You absolutely should keep such a file. The whole job hunting process is messy and confusing at times and keeping everything in ship shape from the start will save you a lot of time. So do it, and do it from the beginning. It's balls-achingly dull when you have that epiphany moment (usually precipitated by invitation to interview) and decide to get with the program but then have to scrat and rummage around for hours searching for CVs and paperwork you placed in various 'safe places' over the past God knows how many weeks.

*"If I had six hours to chop down a tree, I'd spend the first*
*four sharpening the axe."*
Abraham Lincoln

Clearly Abe was *big* on preparation. But being as having a sharp axe means you can chop quicker, more accurately and with less chance of a blunt edge causing the axe to bounce and hack into your own leg, you can see that it does make sense to take time out to prepare and thus have everything (in his case the axe) prepared for the task ahead.

Frequently the job file recommendations focus on a physical file where you should keep a copy of all the adverts responded to, along with copies of the covering letter, and CV or application form you sent. In short everything relating to your job search. Crucially though don't confine your organisational prowess to physical documents alone. Also create folders on your computer, and within your email inbox. With so much of your job hunt taking place online it's imperative you keep all your job related email exchanges organised. You need to know who you contacted and when, and what documents you sent them (which copy of your CV for example (especially important if you have tailored your CV for a specific role)).

**Fine. But What About the Notebook?** I want you to up the ante, and take this to the next level! A file is all well and good. But you're going for Wow Factor (that deserves capitals I feel). And that's why you need 'The Notebook of Success'. I apologise for the cheesy name, call it your Little Black Book, call it your Job Hunt Bible, call it Bob, Ermintrude, Gert or Frank if you like… just do it. Believe me this single idea will give you such an edge, and yet you can't get ideas much simpler than this. (In answer to the question that may well be in your head this point: *No, this book is not merely full of simple, obvious ideas, however where simple and obvious ideas provide solutions to common problems or provide an opportunity for you to gain an edge over your competition…? Well then, yes, I do point out the ideas so many candidates fail to think of, or, more pertinently, fail to put into practice.*)

Get yourself, or dig out from your desk drawer, a notebook. An old address book (unused(!)) can work well.

For all the agencies you contact note the following: Name of Agency, phone number, website, address, name of RC you have contacted / are dealing with, where you found the agency (newspaper / online / recommendation etc.)

Each time you deal with the agency (from your very first contact) in any capacity (phonecalls, interviews, jobs they put you forward for (even if you didn't get an interview). Jot down the time and date and a shorthand summary of what was involved, and any outcome.

Always always note the date, time and name of any RC involved (you may not be able to speak directly to *your* RC if they're out, are interviewing or are on the phone (Useful shorthand LMTCB = Left Message To Call Back, LMVM = Left Message on Voicemail)).

Whether or not you're using an old address book (which is recommended) allocate a page or two (or more) for each agency (number of pages depends on the size of the book and the size of your handwriting). The entries should be added alphabetically. (Easier in an alphabetically tabbed address book of course.)

**So what's the reason for all this?** Most candidates provide their mobile phone number on their CV or application. RCs then call this number and (going by figures provided by a large number and broad selection of RCs) anything between 20% (not good) and 80% (horrifying) of candidates either don't recall making the application at all, or don't recall which advert they were responding to. You may think *you'll* remember, but please trust me on this. No matter how great your memory is, you *will* have days when you're distracted, days when you'll have emailed several agencies, or responded to several online adverts on a jobsite over a period of a couple of weeks or so and they *will* start to merge into one another. If the very first impression an RC gets on speaking to you, is that you're not even focussed enough or interested enough in the job they're advertising to remember it... well it rather undermines the credibility of the claims in your covering letter regarding your enthusiasm and commitment to being considered for that particular role don't you think?

Even if the RC may have been prepared to cut you some slack (because *of course* they're used to candidates not remembering the details of their application), just imagine what a great impression you'll make when, in the snap of a finger, you're able to have all the information in front of you and be able to converse with them intelligently and confidently about your application. Simply by having this notebook and *crucially* by keeping it with you at all times, you'll stand out from the crowd immediately:  you'll be head and shoulders above your competitors from the get-go.

An extra tip in a similar vein: when you're actively dealing with an agency, enter the phone number in your mobile phone. This is useful for practicalities like alerting them if you're delayed for an interview etc. But don't simply enter the main number you use to phone them; instead when you meet with an RC find out what phone number shows up when they phone you (they may have a specific line and number that is used for outgoing calls). (Of course it may be a switchboard that withholds numbers or shows as 'private', unfortunately neither of these is much use for this recommendation)). Anyway, having the number in your phone means it will flash up on your screen, thus giving you invaluable lead time when an RC calls. So you'll have a chance to get your head into gear *before* you answer the phone, and of course you can pull out your notebook!

Make sure you not only keep the notebook with you at all times, but also have a pen or pencil with you to add new entries. (Personally, for what it's worth, I favour pencils. It's much easier to correct an illegible scribble if it was only in pencil in the first place.)

Your notebook is not supposed to have all the intricate detail of your communications. Just the headlines, or bullet points: all the information you need to know who you're talking to and why you're talking to them. The full details will be in your Job File. I'm sure some of you will be thinking that this is a ridiculous waste of time, and that you're double handling the information. Trust me, the first time you answer your mobile and you are able to use the RC's name and discuss your application with confidence, you'll realise why your notebook is such a simple and yet effective tool. If you don't get yourself a notebook and use it then I'll make a prediction, one of the following will happen, either:

(a) you'll make a bunch of great applications, with stonkingly well constructed covering letters and CVs. A couple of weeks later your mobile will ring when you're out and about. As the RC talks you'll begin to hear and feel your stomach acid gurgling as a feeling of panic washes over your whole body and you wrack your brains to fathom which advert it was that this lovely RC is ringing about. You will go home and start your notebook. Alternatively...

(b) you'll do no such thing. You'll receive a call from an RC, and you'll tough it out. With confidence and panache you'll hide the fact you don't recall the exact advert. You'll end the call feeling rather chuffed with yourself for bluffing your way through it. But... the RC won't have been fooled: bluffer to bluffer they'll have sniffed you out straight away, and you'll have missed your first (direct contact) chance to gain a competitive edge.

**Trust me on the notebook. It's worth it.**

# Chapter Three

# PREPARATION:
# HELPING YOURSELF

*"If you want a glass of milk, you don't sit in the middle of field in the hope that a generous and obliging cow will back up to you and milk herself"*

The above may sound preposterous, and yet an astonishing number of candidates aren't even *that* focussed: honestly... really... some candidates don't even make the decision they want milk. And can you imagine how stupid you'd feel sitting in that field for days on end only to realise you wanted lemonade all along? Now let's move along before we milk <boom boom> that poor metaphor to death.

If landing your ideal job was easy, let's face it, you'd already have done it. The bad (but predictable) news is that it's far from easy. The good news is that time invested in good ground work (preparation) will vastly reduce the potential for time wasted ahead and will radically increase the efficacy of all your actions.

*In short: minutes and hours invested now will translate into days and weeks saved later.*

In order to handle your RC successfully, you need to know:

**a) What you want:** What industry? What type of role? What industry sector? What specific field? What size of organisation? What position? What level? What prospects? What salary? What package?

**b) Where you want it:** What location? Would you like to join an organisation with offices in other parts of the country, or other parts of the world with a view to moving to other offices later in your career?

**c) When you want it:** What's your timescale? What deadlines have you set yourself? What deadlines are imposed on you by circumstances you can't control? (Circumstances such as financial or personal/family commitments.) By what date would you aim to have secured a new role? You must set yourself a timescale for the whole process with goals and deadlines for each stage. Only you can assess how much time (and money) can pass through your hands before you have to have found a new job.

**d) Why you want all of the above?** This one sounds as though it's in danger of verging on self indulgent navel-gazing. But that couldn't be further from the truth. You really need to know *why* you want the things you want. What's your motivation? Are you looking for substantial financial reward? Self respect? Prestige? Job satisfaction? Office camaraderie? A happy and relaxed working life? A junior position that will provide you with a launch pad for your glittering career? A job with flexible hours close to home and your childcare facilities? The possibilities verge on endless. Only *you* know what's driving and motivating your job search. But, truly, as hippy and self indulgent as it may seem, you do need to take the time to work this out. It's only when you've done this, that you'll be able to effectively identify your search parameters and rate your demands in order of importance. (That last part is vital because unless you're very *very* **very** lucky you'll never get *everything* you're looking for in a job.)

**e) How are you going to go about it:** See the previous chapter and make your own final decision. However (predictably) I'd recommend making the most of RCs. You don't necessarily have to use them in isolation, but certainly as one of your weapons in your assault on the job market.

**"Nice idea in theory but I don't have that kind of time"**
Now, you may be thinking:
*"That's all well and good Herbie. And I agree that in an ideal world one would research and prepare and all that. But this is the real world, I'm already working all hours to pay the bills and what time I have left is filled with:*
(Tick all that apply)
□ *overtime*   □ *commuting*   □ *my kids / family*
□ *studying*   □ *laundry*   □ *housework*   □ *flat / house hunting*
□ *cooking*   □ *gym/working out*   □ *my dog / cat / snake*
□ *all the necessities that I have no choice about doing or not!*
□ *actually having 'a life': dating / socialising... which includes networking which is good for finding a job anyway, so there!*
□ *obvious other things you haven't even thought of Herbie!!!"*

OK. Deep breath. Calm down. Got all that out of your system? Good. Sitting comfortably? Because I'm about to raise your blood pressure with an influx of clichés you probably won't like either:

- ↳ Failing to prepare is preparing to fail.
- ↳ If you want something done ask a busy person.
- ↳ Or maybe you think it's about luck? ...Well it's amazing how the harder you work (at researching and preparing for your job search), the 'luckier' you get...
- ↳ Think of it like this: if your life seems almost too hard to handle, and you want a new job but you feel you haven't got time to faff around with all this introspective BS, remember the old jar metaphor (I'm anticipating you will have heard a version of this before, but will you just humour me anyway and read to the end?):

Imagine you've got a big empty jar (this jar represents your day), and you fill it to the top with rocks about 2" in diameter. They represent your family, your health, your friends etc. Is the jar full? No of course not. Now take some pebbles and pour them into the jar. Jiggle the jar around. The pebbles will, of course, end up plopping into spaces between the rocks. Let's say the pebbles represent your job, your overtime, your extra studying etc. Then of course you've got all that stuff you *have* to do everyday; commute, shop, laundry, etc. Let's represent that with sand. Pour the sand over the top. Jiggle the jar. Press the sand down hard. Force every possible grain into that jar. *Now* is the jar full? What do you reckon? Next (in your imagination) pour out a drink of your choice. Ideally your absolute favourite. Beer? Martini? Wine? Mix yourself a Margarita? Coke? 7UP? Water? Juice? Now imagine pouring that into the jar. Will it fit? Of course it will. Because as the punchline goes, 'There's always room for beer'. OK, so the beer is obviously your research and preparation so just do it will you? For your own sake?! Now, please will you put down that metaphorical drink, this is no time for boozing, you've got an RC to handle!

**Time spent in research and preparation is NOT wasted.**
*Time wasted* is the time (and nervous energy) spent preparing for job interviews that turn out to be totally wrong for you.
*Time wasted* is time spent having to explain to an RC that you're not interested in the sorts of roles they keep phoning you about.
*Time wasted* is time spent phoning and emailing an RC who never

returns your calls or emails and when they do, seems to have forgotten who you are and what you're looking for.

*Time wasted* is time spent reminding such an RC of the parameters of your search, and of the correct or best ways to contact you.

*Time wasted* is time spent explaining to your Boss (who doesn't know you're looking for a new job) why you're getting calls and emails at the office from a certain RC. (And why are you getting such calls at work? Because you haven't handled your RC correctly, and they're all over the place!)

All that, and more, is *time wasted*.

**OK. So let's look at two basic questions:**
   **1) Where are you now?**
   **2) Where do you want to be?**

**1) WHERE ARE YOU NOW?**
Quite possibly, on the tube... in the bath, on a bus, on your sofa, at your desk... but obviously that's not quite what I meant. I meant where are you jobwise? I've split the below into two (first jobbers and new jobbers) but pick and choose to see what applies to you.

**If you're looking for your first job or returning to work:** What's your timescale? When do you intend to have started a new role? What are your key pressures? Time? Money? Outside pressures (eg Parental pressure? Partner pressure? Peer pressure? Emotional pressure (eg depressed at not working)?) What's your current financial situation? Is this new job intended to be the first step on the rung of a very long ladder? Is it simply a means to an end? (eg A chance to get some experience and then set up on your own?) What do you want from this job? The security of a regular income? Potential for career progression? Opportunity to make a great deal of money? Chance to learn about an industry and build a new career?

**If you're currently employed:** Why are you looking for a new role? Are you looking to change location? Position? Industry? Salary? Looking for career progression? Develop your role? Find a better cultural fit (AKA get away from the office eejits/unreasonable boss you can't stand)? Have you explored any possibilities for progression or lateral movement within your current organisation? Does your employer know you are looking for a new role? Do you intend to alert your employer to your search prior to actually giving notice? What's your timescale? When do you anticipate being out of where you are and in somewhere new? What's your notice period? Do you anticipate working your notice or does your organisation typically ask you to clear your desk once notice has been given? When do you intend to give notice? Are you planning to give notice only on securing a concrete offer? Are you keen to leave as soon as possible? (NOTE: Don't make rash decisions on  this front, the old adage about it being better to look for a new job from the security of an existing one, often holds true.)

## 2)WHERE DO YOU WANT TO BE?

The latter part of this section is split into three parts: Ideals, Realities & Practicalities. All are key and I really can't emphasise enough how important it is that you give sufficient weight to them all. You see, whilst knowing what you are aiming for is vital, (and trust me, I am not discouraging you from aiming for the stars) knowing your value in the marketplace is absolutely imperative. All RCs I spoke to in the course of researching and compiling this book cited tales of candidates whose job expectations (usually salary, sometimes level) were wholly unrealistic, who were consequently impossible to place as no job was ever good enough.

So please, listen to me. You need to ascertain what's important to you, and what you want. But, you MUST also ascertain what's important to the market and what the market wants.

*Know the marketplace and your value within it.*

So how do you ascertain your value? We'll come to that later in this chapter. But don't rely solely on your RC for this information. It's natural, and indeed important, for you to ask your RC questions. But remember they are not there as a career advisor, or life coach, nor are they in many cases as well informed as they could or should be. Having said all that a good RC will indeed be able to give you some idea of your value in the marketplace, and of the state of the market in general. But a mediocre, or even lousy RC, will either refuse to take a stab at your value, or will have a go but make it up as they go along: neither of which are of any value to you.

Whether they have the answers or not, remember you shouldn't be relying on your RC as the sole provider of that information.

You should be knowledgeable about the market you want to enter. If you aren't then you haven't prepared properly. Plus, if you stop and think about it: if you're relying on your RC's assessment alone (or give the impression that you are), then what happens if it transpires that your expectations are higher than *their* assessment of what you can expect? Frankly you'll have left yourself without a leg to stand on when it comes to arguing your case. (A case for a better job with more money.)

By all means ask them. It will aid you in assessing their skills, experience and knowledge. But only ask them when you are prepared, so that you can turn to turn it into a discussion of the state of the market, and your value within that marketplace. They should not be *telling* you your value, however a discussion between two well informed people is an entirely different proposition.

♫ NOTE: When asked "What are your salary expectations?"
The answer "As much as possible" or variants on it, are tired and overused. When delivered with a cheeky smile they can raise a smirk, but the answer is a poor one, only usable if immediately followed with a proper, well considered answer that is backed up with properly researched data.

## IDEALS

This is ideals as in *achievable ideals*, so we're not talking: *'Ideally I'd like to be a formula one champion with £50million in the bank, a Bugatti Veyron, an island in the Caribbean and my own personal sushi chef'*

...instead we're talking more: *'I'd like to be working in a small to medium sized hedge fund, central London based, ideally Mayfair, in a mid level administrative position offering potential for growth, earning circa £32k plus a performance related bonus.'*

Remember, no job will ever satisfy all your needs and desires. I'm not being a pessimist, I'm being a realist, if you go out there into the marketplace with a fantastical notion for a dream job, those dreams will be crushed. Set your sights on a realistic goal; it may be a tough one (tough can be good(!)), but just make it realistic.

**Ideal Industry:** In what industry, and specifically industry sector, do you want to work?

**Ideal Position/Level:** What sort of position would you like to move into, be it a first job, or moving on in your career?

**Ideal Location:** Where do you want to work?

**Salary:** How much would you like to earn (being sensible about it), and (being sensible) is this the same as the amount you genuinely anticipate you could earn?

## REALITIES

**Industry, the realities:** Are you qualified, skilled or experienced in the industry or field you wish to work in?

**Position/Level, the realities:** How do you compare to the candidates already in the marketplace who are also seeking the positions you want?

**Location, the realities:** Are there opportunities at your level in that location? Can you realistically relocate if you need to?

**Salary, the realities:** How much do people with your skills and experience, working in that industry averagely earn?

## PRACTICALITIES

**Industry, the practicalities:** Are there many, or any, jobs in that industry or industry sector, available for candidates of your calibre and experience?

**Position/Level, the practicalities:** How often do jobs at your level in that industry become available?

**Location, the practicalities:** Do you currently live near enough to the location you want to work in? If not can you afford to relocate?

**Salary, the practicalities:** Will your likely salary be enough (after travel costs etc) to allow you live in the area you've chosen? Will the salary you can realistically expect to earn fund your lifestyle? If not, is it likely to increase in a workable time frame, and do you have savings or some source of financial support that can tide you over in the meantime? Alternatively can you adapt your lifestyle to mean you can live within your means?

## SO. WHAT ARE YOU WORTH?
### How do you ascertain your market value?

We're going to go into a lot of depth about researching your RCs and agencies in Chapter Seven. However, happily, the research you need to carry out to ascertain your market value overlaps with that research: see you're saving time already!

I once had an economics lecturer who was inordinately fond of the old maxim:   ***How much is anything worth?***
***As much as a given person is prepared to pay***
***at a given time.***
And it does of course make sense... even if it is a little airy fairy and lacking in quick and concrete guidance.

Essentially your research to establish your market value, is simply your way of assessing just that, ie: what a given person might realistically be prepared to pay at a given time for 'You'.

Read. Talk. Listen. Question. Quiz. Brain pick.

 ᠔ Read industry publications (online or in print). Back issues from the last 12 months are recent enough to have relevance (unless there's been a major industry shake up). Articles about skills shortages and salaries often crop up. Most importantly trawl the job advertisements in these publications and identify jobs you think you would genuinely have a chance of landing (NOTE: *genuinely* ie realistically, not jobs that you could get 'if only' ie 'if only you had the experience they've asked for', or 'if only you had at least a 2.1 in Engineering'.) Note what salaries (or salary ranges)and packages they are offering.

 ᠔ Read national and local press. Ascertain what days the sort of jobs you're looking for are advertised in the various newspapers. Search the adverts, and editorial as above.

 ᠔ Trawl the websites of organisations in the industry. Do they have a careers section, if so do they give an indication of packages or salaries?

 ᠔ Seek out salary surveys. Agencies that specialise in specific industries or industry sectors often carry out salary surveys. These are useful, though do not rely on them in isolation, instead use them in conjunction with your other research. (I've witnessed such surveys involve nothing more than a senior RC taking a vox pop around the office).

 ᠔ Check out jobsites and agency websites.

 ᠔ Speak to people in (or who know about) the industry.

 ᠔ If still at University (or have only recently left): speak to careers advisors, lecturers and tutors. Find out if they know people working in the industry who they could ask on your behalf, or (even better for networking) put you in touch with to speak to directly. Also check your alumni database to see if there are any alumni it may be worth contacting.

ᕽ Pick the brains of family and friends, either for their own knowledge or to be put in touch with their contacts.

ᕽ When you look at the packages and figures being bandied about bear in mind any location related weighting. (For example: London based jobs in organisations with offices across the country often (though not always) list salaries with a weighting to reflect the additional cost of living in the capital.)

The above suggestions are not listed in order of importance, and the how much useful data you'll gather from each source will vary widely.

Once you've built up a clear picture of your market value and have realistic expectations based on the current market, then you're ready to launch yourself into that market and actively seek your new role. But do make sure you keep abreast of any developments. Your research will become dated over time, and new issues will arise; for example new skills shortages. And when such things occur you need to know about them, because only then will you be in a position to capitalise on them.

When you carry out this research it's really important you get it right. There are a number of pitfalls which will mean you get it very wrong. Don't take any single piece of information at face value. And don't use any one method of research in isolation. Particularly beware of using that special sort of logic we're all prone to using at times. You know, something akin to: *"Donkey's exist. I exist. Therefore I am a donkey."*

Or in job terms: *"I went to Uni with Joe Bloggs. I know I'm smarter than Joe. I'm brighter than Joe. In fact let's face it I'm quicker witted, funnier and better company than Joe. Joe's package is worth about £37,000. I've been out for a drink with Joe and Joe told me all about the job. I know I could do it with my eyes closed, in fact I could do it so easily I'd probably be bored. Therefore I am worth £37,000. At least."*

No. Just no. Listen to yourself. Who are you trying to kid? If you *do* want to use Joe as a tool or measure in your research try asking yourself these questions and more: How do your academic qualifications compare to Joe's? Your work experience? Is that an industry sector that interests you? How long has Joe been working there or in that industry? Do you currently work in that (or a similar) industry? Honestly, would you actually want Joe's job?

Such mistakes, or silly deductions, can easily lead to you overestimating your market value (or indeed in some cases underestimating, though funnily enough this is a far less frequent occurrence). Such over estimations are a huge source of frustration for RCs, but *they* aren't my primary concern *you* are. And I want to make sure that (a) you don't set yourself up for a fall and (b) you don't get off to a bad start with your RC by seeming to be ill informed, egotistical and arrogant, and (potentially) a candidate who's going to waste their time with an unrealistic wish list.

Just from my own recent experience, at the time of writing I can think of three individuals, all of whom are decent/good candidates on paper.  But *all* of them are still searching for jobs (using several  different RCs), because they're pitching for jobs that are completely out of their league and they refuse to accept that they rate themselves more highly than the market does. I know that sounds harsh, and is only one step away from saying they aren't quite as good or clever (or experienced) as they think they are, but their problems finding jobs are self inflicted.  Ironically, one of the candidates keeps raising his salary requirements! His explanation: "The longer I'm out of work, the more I need to earn to pay off my increasing debts". No amount of reasoning (by me (and believe me I am actually capable of being jolly persuasive at times) or his other RCs) seems to communicate to him how illogical and unrealistic this is... I mean he can't get a job because he's looking for too much money and now he wants more?!?!?

## IN SUMMARY: BE PREPARED

*You need to have all the answers to all the above questions, so that you can manage, control, and HANDLE your RC.* You need to ensure your RC understands you, and your job search.  You're the only person that can make that happen. And let's face it, if *you* don't know what you want, how can you possibly explain it to your RC?  To paraphrase (and truncate) the infamous Scout motto (Robert Baden-Powell, Scouting for Boys, 1908):

**"BE PREPARED which means you must always be in a state of readiness in mind and body to handle your RC"**

# Chapter Four

# THINK RC:
# TWO MOONS IN HIS MOCCASINS

*"Judge not a man until you have walked two moons in his moccasins"*
*Somewhat overused and clichéd (allegedly Native American) proverb*

Now you don't have to read this chapter, you could go skipping along to Chapter Four, but WAIT! Before you race off, just hold fire little puppy ...just for one second... because if you elect not to read this chapter (and after all it's not very long) you'll be missing a trick. Obviously this chapter isn't about footwear, and I'm not going to use the tired old punchline to the above proverb (you know the one... "Because that way if he doesn't like what you've got to say you're two moons away and you've got his shoes" ...OK so I *have* sort of just used it but I digress...). If you really want to know how to handle someone you need to understand them. I'm not talking deep and meaningful touchy feely stuff, just a decent, commonsensical and basic grasp of who you're dealing with and how they function. Because once you've got a handle on all that...? Well, *then* you're in tip top prime position to handle them to your advantage.

You need to get a grasp on how RCs think and how they work. Don't worry, although my own experiences are (of course!) crammed full of juicy, useful and relevant content I'm not arrogant enough to rely on that alone (I've leave the unenviable trait of arrogance to the lousy RCs... they do it so well). The driving force behind the creation of this chapter is that it became apparent during the course of researching this book (a process I immersed myself into so wholeheartedly that I was up to my armpits in RCs and candidates sharing their pearls of wisdom, and even found myself dreaming about them), just how much misunderstanding there is in the relationship between candidates and RCs.

## WHY DO THEY NEED 'HANDLING' WHY DON'T THEY JUST GET ON WITH THEIR FLIPPING JOB AND WORK FOR YOU?

Crux of the issue is that they don't work for *you*, that *isn't* their job. They work for their employer (the agency) and they work for their client; who is of course your potential employer.

**THE CURATE'S EGG:** The reality is that yes, agencies are client driven. They want to source the best possible candidates for their clients. But do remember, it's not a one way street: whilst *you* need *them* to sell you to their client (so you can go for that job you so desperately want), *they* also need *you* in order to earn their commission by filling that job. The annoying part, where the relationship is a little less fairly balanced? Whilst you want that job really badly, in all reality there are other candidates out there who they could probably place in that job instead of you (and who would still get them their commission). Now that of course is not always the case. In certain markets the lack of really good candidates with the right skills means that the candidate is much more in control. But for most people the truth is that they're not the only candidate out there who can do the job and do it well. So truth is that not only are you *not* the client, but to add insult to injury they don't regard you as irreplaceable. (Though as you'll discover, one of the fundamental tenets of handling your RC is to make them rate you highly, thus edging you somewhat further towards the 'irreplaceable' end of the hypothetical candidate value scale RCs seem to unconsciously have in their heads.)

## SO IS THAT IT?  IS IT JUST ABOUT COMMISSION? AM I MERELY A WALKING £ (POUND SIGN)?

Yes and no. Look let's be realistic RCs aren't aid workers or charity volunteers, and generally speaking they're not doing this job solely out of the good of their hearts. They have bills and mortgage payments or rent to pay just like you. So of course money plays a part. Having said that no RC worth his salt should ever make you feel as though you are merely a walking £ sign.

In fact if the RC plays their cards right you're much *more* than merely a £ sign... you're a walking cash cow. No, I'm kidding. Well sort of... because in reality if they place you in a great job that you love, then in all likelihood you'll go on to recommend them to others, you may ensure that RC gets first dibs on new positions that your new organisation is seeking to fill and you may return to them in a few years time if and when you're looking to move on. All of which generates income for that RC.

In short, you could potentially put a decent amount of business their way. But yes, they do need that immediate commission; a hefty whack of their pay cheque often relies on it. So to some RCs you are, in the crudest possible interpretation: a means to an end, as some have been known to say 'a walking £ (or $) sign'.

## OK, WELL WHAT *DO* THEY EARN? THE TRUTH.

This is clearly entering the land of generalisations but let's persevere anyway. For most RCs their salary is made up of (in the majority of cases) a rather paltry basic salary plus a performance related commission. In simple terms a common structure is this: if an RC places a candidate with a client, the client pays the agency a big juicy fee (in many cases anything from 15% to 25% of the new employee's first year's salary). Note: it's the agency that gets the juicy fee, and not the consultant.

RCs usually have monthly or quarterly targets they must hit before they receive commission. Targets vary wildly; £8k.. £20k... £50k... many variables drive it. When (and only when) the target is hit the RC will get a percentage of the fee; their commission. Percentages can be as little as 5% or as much as 100% in some cases. However, often the commission is split between more than one RC. The commission may be pooled, then shared amongst a whole office, or it may be split amongst a specific team, or it may be allocated 50/50 (75/25, 60/40 etc) between the consultant who first brought the client on board and the consultant who registered you (the candidate). The calculation will be seemingly simple, yet in reality headache inducingly complex. In the end the commission earned probably isn't anything like as much as you imagine when you grumble into your glass of wine or pint that they're all a bunch of you-know-whats and it's money for old rope.

## WHY DO THEY BECOME RCs?

You may well have seen adverts both in print media and online, offering fairly enticing packages. You may even have been tempted to apply. Of course your RC may well have applied for their job based on just such an advert. A classic example would be:

---

**Graduate Financial Recruitment Consultant**

Want to earn 60K in your first year?

Recruitment isn't for everyone but for those who can rise to the challenge the rewards are worth it! So if you're competitive, driven, self-motivated, self-sufficient, resilient and patient with bags of stamina we want to hear from you. Graduates only. 2.2 and above. Good University. No recruitment experience required.

OTE £60K in first year, OTE £80K in second year

Generous Basic + Comm + Pension + Team Rewards

---

I'll be blunt, of the many RCs I have known, worked with, interviewed and impertinently quizzed about their earnings; I have yet to come across an RC with no recruitment experience who has genuinely earned £60k in their first year. I mention this so that you don't feel resentful that they're getting rich off your back, because believe me most of them aren't. And in that advert above where it lists generous basic? To put that into perspective I've spoken to RCs whose 'Generous Basic' is as little as £12k.

Note: you may be interested to know that it is pretty common practice for RCs to be contractually prohibited from discussing their salary and commission structure, in some contracts it is actually a dismissable offence. Why you may ask? Those who draw up such contracts argue that it is to prevent any jealousy or conflict amongst team members who may have negotiated different basics or commission structures. Personally being a natural cynic I can't help but think that two of the driving motivations are:

(1) To ensure that they get their consultants for the best possible price; ie the lowest basic and smallest commission. (After all if they all clubbed together RCs could try to force an employer's hand on the pay structure... an RC's cartel if you will).

(2) A slight element of 'divide and conquer', after all if an RC believes some of their colleagues may be being paid more than them but they also believe they are being paid more than others, then the RCs are likely to enjoy the one-upmanship be more discreet about their earnings and secretly find their competitive urges stoked (to catch up and overtake the others).

That said, the money is often a motivation for becoming an RC. Rumour has it, and some people have found it to be true, that if you're good at your job, in recruitment you'll find that your remuneration will reflect that. Now it's tricky to say whether or not this is always the case, for starters not everyone has the same interpretation of 'being good at their job'. Is it placing a large number of candidates regardless of whether they really like the job you've found them? Personally I don't think it is. But to give you some idea of how the person sitting in the agency peering at you over their desk actually got there I've included a brief list of some of the answers I got when researching this book:

1) "I sort of fell into it." (NB: this was THE most popular answer.)

2) "I wanted a career that offered the chance to progress, but that provided decent training, opportunities to transfer to overseas

offices, and would give me a chance to prove myself despite having no relevant experience"

3) "Can't remember why. But there again I don't know anyone who actually set out to work in recruitment."

4) "I'd graduated and needed a job but didn't know quite what to do, so I applied for this. But at the end of the day I've ended up finding nice people nice jobs for a living. That's not so bad is it?"

5) "I qualified as a solicitor but hated law. Had a rethink. Figured I like working with people, and recruitment is supposed to be all about working with people."

6) "I'd been in media sales, and an estate agent so anything was a step up."

7) "I'd been in the civil service and was bored. Wanted the chance to interact with people, build business relationships and earn more money."

8) "Liked the idea of being paid on performance without having to do cold calling. Although actually now ironically I have to do loads of cold calling."

9) And last but not least a rather sweet one: "I loved the idea of it; finding people jobs. Matching people with organisations. Changing peoples lives. OK so I was a bit over optimistic and dewy eyed. The reality is rather less fairy tale like, but I still love it."

So as you can see from the tiny sample above there are a lot of reasons your RC has ended up sat at their desk. And ironically for an industry that prides itself on placing the right people in the right jobs, none of those reasons (with the exception of the last) suggests those people really wanted to be RCs. That's probably one of the reasons staff turnover in the industry is so notoriously high. It's difficult to gather accurate data on this as there is not a central licensing authority or body; but some say its as high as 40% which is true in some firms. In short your RC may not have handled their own job search with any great skill. *You* have to be the brains of the organisation as far as *your* job search goes. They have advantages you need to make the most of; their contacts, their access to decision makers, their influence, their database, the jobs on their books, their inside track knowledge of jobs that may be coming up soon. But please engrave it in your mind:

**YOU ARE THE BRAINS OF THE ORGANISATION**

(the 'Organisation' being: Getting You A Great Job Inc.)

**A NECESSARY EVIL?**

## OH COME ON! HAVE A HEART… (AND A BRAIN…)

A common observation RCs have made to them is that they are a necessary evil.   Now I don't know about you but being called 'an evil' necessary or otherwise doesn't inspire me to feel affection or any feelings of positivity at all towards to the person spouting off. RCs (generally speaking) do get a bum rap. I'm not going to give you a sob story, far from it.  There are some useless unscrupulous slimeballs out there calling themselves RCs who fully deserve your disdain.  All I want you to do is bear in mind how easy it is to fall into the trap of being vile about *all*  RCs and  finding yourself treating them all accordingly, and in turn how damaging that can be to your own interests.

> Sam an RC, the morning after being ridiculed and verbally mauled at a dinner party after revealing she was in recruitment:  *"Why on earth do people hate recruiters so much?  We find people jobs for God's sake… isn't that a worthwhile thing to spend your day doing?!?!  I mean it makes people happy… it means they can pay their bills… sustain themselves without being a drain on society…  it means they pay taxes… which pay for schools …and hospitals or at least goes towards the woefully underfunded NHS and all that s\*\*t… it keeps the whole godamned economy going… and keeps \*$%@s like him in work."*

Now I accept she is arguably overstating her case, but you can't help but see her point. And that wrath isn't simply the preserve of drunken dinner party guests… families get in there too… (though it seems embarrassment is the driving force here…)

> *"Shortly after my fiancé and I went to the registry office (to give notice of our intent to marry), my mother and I ended up in the most absurd stand up row.  She was mortified that I'd put 'Recruitment Consultant' down as my occupation.  She kept raging on and on about how it would haunt me forever and be there on my marriage certificate for everyone to see.  She kept ranting how she'd have preferred me to have put anything else.  She'd probably even have preferred mass murderer.  It was ridiculous and hurtful, though on the murderer side of things I admit matricide seemed a fleetingly appealing option."*
> Emily,  IT Recruitment Consultant

*"Not long after I started my first recruitment job a candidate
likened me, as a recruitment consultant, to* <insert name of
huge and notorious chain of fast food burger joints> *and*
<insert name of large and somewhat brash London estate
agents with distinctively decorated small vehicles>: *'You're
like ----- and -----, no one likes you or wants to use you
but in the end we end up having to come to you... you're a
sort of necessary evil.' Needless to say I didn't go out of my
way to find this t\*\*t a job; I had \*\*\*\*loads of nicer more
personable people on my books that I actually gave a stuff
about. I got them great jobs!"*      Dan, Financial Sector RC

Let's face it when you stop and think about it not only is it unfair to
treat all RCs as bottom feeding scum suckers but also if you treat
them like that you're just shooting yourself in the foot.

And let's not forget that whilst there are lousy RCs, by the same
token you get lousy examples of people in all walks of life. I bet
you've come across lousy examples of one or more of the following:
teachers, doctors, nurses, builders, plumbers, dentists, secretaries,
managers, actors, IT Consultants, singers, artists (Turner Prize
Winners anyone?), politicians, lawyers, hairdressers (you should
see what some of them have done to my hair in the past... it brings
a tear to my eye just thinking about it), mechanics, dentists... the
list goes on and on.

But not all teachers, doctors or singers etc are lousy are they?
You wouldn't lump Harold Shipman (GP & Serial Killer, though
I suspect the latter wasn't on his business or calling cards) and
Dr Christiaan N Barnard (surgeon who performed first heart
transplant) in the same category would you? So do yourself a
favour and apply that same logic to RCs; don't tar them all with
the same brush lumping them all into the 'lousy' category.

OK, well my soapbox is feeling rather rickety now after jumping
up and down on it for a whole chapter so let's wrap this up and
move on. In a nutshell, the fact that RCs get so much aggravation
and negativity from so many people means you can get off to a
flying start in your relationship with yours by not treating them
this way. Easy enough really don't you think?

## Chapter Five

# BEING HANDLED:
# HOW RCs TRY TO HANDLE *YOU*

In reality all RCs want to be able to handle their candidates, though they often confuse this with control (see the point below). This is a mistake in my opinion, as generally speaking people don't like to feel they're being controlled. I know it brings out the worst in me. Imagine a small puppy on a lead for the first time, if you try to *control* him and just tug hard on the lead he'll almost certainly whack his bottom straight to the floor, dig his front paws and little claws hard into the ground (or carpet... or (eeks) wooden flooring) and do his darnedest to stay rooted to the spot. However if you *handle* the same puppy intelligently, and introduce the idea of the lead, coax him, encourage him and communicate with him, chances are he'll trot alongside you merrily.

Most RCs have their own 'secret' little bag of tricks for handling their candidates. But there are a number of common techniques that are exceptionally popular right across the board, and it is those that I present to you here.

## CONTROL THE CANDIDATE:
## THE MUCH LOVED RC MANTRA

From here to Timbuktu in agencies across the land the cry of 'control your candidates' is uttered from the lips of managers on a daily basis. The RCs genuinely believe that (a) you are controllable and that (b) *they're* capable of controlling you.

You should disabuse them of those beliefs early on. But don't do it in a bolshy fashion; that'll just get their backs up. Instead you need to be more subtle than that. You need to communicate to them that you're both on the same side, or 'team' if you like. Communicate that you're working towards the same goal. Which after all is true, you are: you both want *you* to get a good job that you love and are happy in. *You* want it for obvious reasons, and *they* want it for the commission and also because it's their job to get you a great job; so there's the whole job satisfaction thing for them thrown in there too.

It's pretty obvious why they want to control you; they believe it makes their lives easier. I don't believe it does. Controlling suggests that one party has the upper hand, and that's not a comfortable relationship... unless you're the one with the upper hand!

You need to nip their intention to control you in the bud. The only way to do this is to be so professional and so informed about the market and your own market value that you're not looking to them for guidance and direction. Instead you look to them to provide you with the *opportunities* (ie interviews with potential employers) to attain your market value in the fields you have already identified. If you don't give them direction, they'll take their own and push you down the path that suits them. In some cases this can result in a happy coincidence, as they'll be good enough at their job to match you to a job they want to fill, but you'll greatly increase the likelihood of this happening if you give them proper guidance as to what it is that you actually want from them.

Offer them the chance to be in control, and they'll take it. And once they're in control any attempt to by you to take it back will result in an ungainly power struggle, or simply in them losing interest in you, because they'll regard you as 'difficult'. So avoid ending up in this situation in the first place: know your own mind, be clear about your direction and communicate effectively, thereby ensuring that both you and your RC are 'singing from the same hymn sheet' or some such cheesy metaphor.

Remember I am not suggesting you ignore their advice, after all any RC worth their salt should be able to provide you with useful insights and market knowledge. But you have to be working from a point of strength, ie building on your existing base of knowledge and understanding, not just listening and accepting everything they say like a directionless, empty-headed numbnut.

## MANAGING EXPECTATIONS

Another reason you need to know the market yourself and not merely rely on the RCs is the whole 'managing expectations' swizz. OK, I'll grant you that 'swizz' may seem to be too strong a term, but some RCs do abuse this practice. The motivation behind managing expectations is to make sure the candidate has realistic expectations of the market, and of course of their RC. After all if you, the candidate, expects something the RC cannot or does not deliver, then you will be disappointed.

So, to a point, they are right to manage your expectations. They should make clear what the current state of play is, in terms of; the market in their opinion, your value in the market (again in their opinion) and the time frame for achieving your goals through them, based on their knowledge of the jobs on their books and their business (incoming business and placements) in recent months. They should be able to provide you with a perspective that you (obviously) cannot have yourself, after all they see the jobs and the candidates that are available on a daily basis.

Where it gets a little screwy, is when RCs try to manage your expectations down, so that you will be happily surprised when they get you a better job and better package than you were expecting (and sooner than you were expecting) based on their predictions. Or when you aren't disappointed when nothing happens: because they had told you it was a tough market/quiet market/quiet time around Christmas/Easter/Summer Holidays/New Year/End of Year/Start of School Year etc (delete as applicable).

The other way it gets abused (and the way I had in mind when I used the word swizz) is when RCs plump up your prospects, and give you the impression that they'll have no problem finding you a new job. Those RCs that do this, do so both to convince you that there's no need for you to register with any other RCs (thereby preventing you (and their commission) from being whisked from under their noses by an RC who does have a great job for you) and they are also puffing themselves up and exaggerating their success. (They may do this to impress you, or because they believe it themselves, or because it's a little self-massage for their ego.)

## THE PHANTOM JOBS

OK, so you always suspected they existed. You know the ones; those fabulous jobs that are advertised and yet when you try to apply the RC convinces you the job has 'literally just been put on hold this morning' or 'the client has literally just filled it internally' (RCs are rather fond phrases such as 'literally just' in these circumstances; I think it's in part thanks to the immediacy that's suggested ... they feel it gets them off the hook.)

The fact is that some agencies *do* leave up adverts for great jobs that they've already filled, or that are no longer available. Generally speaking it's thanks to one of the following three reasons:

**1) Forgetfulness, plain and simple:**
They've forgotten to take it down. Truly it's a simple as that. There's nothing underhand about it. It's just been forgotten.

**2) They want you, and they want you badly!**
Rather like certain London Estate Agents who are notorious for

leaving properties on their websites (even after exchange) in the hope of luring in new buyers, some agencies do leave old adverts for great jobs listed on their sites for you to stumble across and hopefully respond to.  In all likelihood the advert  in question will have been for a really sexy job/funky organisation/juicy role/ exciting buzzy industry etc, and it attracted some great candidates. So now, even though the job has gone, they want to attract more candidates of that calibre so that when new jobs come in they've got a stable of great candidates ready and waiting to go.

**3) Posturing and profile:**
The reality is that agencies want and need to impress both candidates and clients. And if an advert (albeit an out of date one) makes a potential client aware of a high profile job the agency has worked on, that may land them business.  Similarly such adverts raise the profile of an agency in the minds of candidates who are flicking through the industry press, or surfing careers sites or relevant industry websites. And then of course there's the rather more earthy posturing; the muscle flexing, groin thrusting element of the recruitment industry that leads certain agencies to want to try and create the impression that they're bigger, stronger and more successful than they actually are, and (with a little luck) slightly rattle their competitors. (The latter rarely works; and certain smaller agencies that leap to mind simply have a reputation amongst their competitors for running bulls\*\*t ads for old jobs.)

I'd love to be able to say that no reputable agency would ever deliberately advertise a non-existent post, but it's too strong a statement for me to make realistically, and I couldn't possibly back it up. What I can say though, is that based on my research and experience, I'm *unaware* of any reputable agencies advertising completely non-existent posts.

**'No job yet' job adverts:** RCs do sometimes place adverts for positions despite the fact the client has not yet 100% agreed to give the RC the business (ie: let them recruit for the job).  However RCs do this because they want to have some great candidates ready, to wow the client (either for when the RC does land the business or to dangle a carrot in front of an undecided and wavering client). (Or as one of my erstwhile colleagues, one prone to malapropisms, once said in a client email "tangle a carrot" (?!?!?) (and no she didn't get the business) though once on the phone she claimed to "dribble a carrot"... which I've always suspected would be an unappealing prospect, and is inarguably a less convincing metaphor, yet to her credit she did in fact get the business.)

Of course sometimes RCs simply place generic adverts to attract candidates for roles in a industry, field or organisation they regular recruit for. This is not the same as phantom jobs, although can lead to candidates getting frustrated when they haven't realised the advert is not for one specific role, with a specific salary etc, and with no immediate prospect of placement.

Now you've had confirmation that phantom job adverts do exist you may be tempted to try and tease information out of your RC. Or worse go at it like a Jack Russell Terrier and keep yapping and snapping away to get them to admit it. My advice? Don't bother. If you're anything like me you're naturally inquisitive, in fact I'm far worse than that: I hate people knowing things I don't know for sure, but about which I have very strong suspicions... (if you get my drift). However in this context even if you're almost certain that the job in question went long before you phoned, or emailed, and you've got a bee in your bonnet that the RC has deliberately tricked you into contacting them about a job they haven't got anymore... you know what? Just let it go.

Fact is, they probably had the job on their books at some stage, so they're likely to have similar jobs in the future. (That is unless it was a one off job and they've lost that client (or the client is now dormant as the RC has fulfilled their only recruitment need)). And do always bear in mind that any explanation they give ("it's just gone" or "I forgot to take it off the site" or "it's on hold" etc) may actually be genuine. If you start getting arsey with them, quizzing them and accusing them, you are in effect calling them a liar. Now, generally speaking, when one person calls another a liar they're not naturally predisposed to do them any favours, and it gets you off to rather a bad start. Instead you should ask if have they have any similar roles and begin to discuss what you're looking for.

So don't get your knickers in a twist about the unfairness of it all, hold your horses and calm down. They're trying to attract good candidates, and whether or not they're going about it in the way that you or I would is really pretty irrelevant. The important thing is that they're keen to attract good candidates like you because they want to be able to place you. That's a very good thing as far as your concerned. And, if their motivation is in part to impress and attract potential clients, those clients are potential employers for you, so again this is a good thing as far as you're concerned. See what I mean? It's really not something to get upset about.

Truth is, that although most consultants spend a lot of their time sifting through shoddily prepared CVs and applications, from utterly inappropriate candidates, they rarely lose an almost childlike hope that a knock out (even an 'ideal') candidate is out there just waiting to be placed by them (and earn them a hefty commission). And in some  weird way you could argue that it makes it almost forgivable (although it's not necessarily the most intelligent way to go about it) for certain agencies to leave up their best adverts. They want to draw in the best candidates, and they're so desperate to impress good candidates and clients that they think it's a good way of doing it.  So to turn this to your advantage: you need to convince them *you* are that knock out candidate... their bright shining hope for the future and their pay packet.

## HOLDING PATTERNS

Not a universally used term, but a common enough technique. Describes a technique or tactic used by RCs to hold onto good candidates even if the agency hasn't got many (or sometimes any) appropriate jobs on their books, or indeed any on the horizon. It can be explained (in part) to many RCs being slightly naive optimists (see above); there's a significant number of them who appear to believe that plenty of new business is just around the corner. So they want to hold on to great candidates and stop them going elsewhere to other RCs who will place them (and get the commission). Thus they believe that if they can keep the candidates in a 'holding pattern' (like planes circling an airport waiting to land (See Page 116)) they'll be able to keep the candidate to themselves and make money (commission) out of them before too long. Of course this is not fair. No matter what they say, register with other RCs and you'll limit the effect this tactic can have on you.

## WHEN IS A NEWBIE NOT A NEWBIE?

In some organisations new RCs are routinely told to give the impression that they are not 'new' to the job, but merely new to that organisation. Now this may enrage you; after all, they're playing with your career opportunities surely?! But truth is that so long as they have been well trained this should be OK. After all, all RCs have to have a handful of candidates who are their 'first candidates'.  It happens, you can't change it, but you'll be pleased to know that it can work to your advantage. (See Page 110 & 111.)

# Chapter Six

# RC SPEAK:
# READING BETWEEN THE LINES
### (Incl: What their adverts say & what they really mean)

In the course of *preparing* to handle, and then *actually* handling your RC you'll be reading *a lot* of job adverts and *a lot* of agency websites. In doing so you're going to come across certain words and phrases time and time again. You may think that there's some hidden meaning, something you should be looking for, or you may be hoping there's a way of eliciting more information than is obvious from the few little sentences in front of you. Well, there is and there isn't, but what there 'is' we'll cover as thoroughly as possible here.

**POINT ONE:** The single most important thing for you to remember when reading adverts written by RCs is this: they are ADVERTISEMENTS. They're sales tools. They're selling a job and a company and the idea of working in that job at that company to you, their potential candidate. So for example let's take something very simple, the salary: an RC is always going to give you the best possible version of the salary in an advert. Therefore when an advert says "Up to £35k", that probably means the client has told them the absolute maximum for the role is £35k, but that will only be paid to the ideal candidate who 'ticks all the boxes', so do not read such an advert and conveniently skip over the 'up to', and end up fixing £35k dead as the salary in your head. And don't assume that's what *you'll* get. Remember all this when talking to them too, RCs are in part salespeople. That's good at times and yet it can be frustrating. It's good when they're selling you to a client. It's frustrating when they're selling a job or client to you that holds no interest for you. However, if you handle them correctly that frustrating part won't happen, because they'll know what you want, why you want it and they'll know not to waste your time and their own.

**POINT TWO:** RCs are not copywriters, many aren't even given formal training in writing adverts. The advert writing lark isn't necessarily their forte and the advert you're reading is likely to be a mish mash of previous adverts they've run before (with a modicum of success) and ones they've seen and liked (written by their colleagues or competitors). Certain words and phrases get massively overused. You know the ones: dynamic, fast-paced, challenging, proactive, creative, self-starter, multi-tasker etc. A useful tip when checking out a single agency's adverts? Look to see if you can identify which RC is responsible for an advert (for example if their email is the contact email for that advert, then they probably wrote it). Now compare it with other adverts of theirs (even for jobs that don't interest you). Now if you find the same words cropping up again and again in their ads, there's a fair chance they're just chuntering and spouting off stock phrases, as it's unlikely all their jobs and clients are so very similar. However if you see words or phrases suggesting urgency, for example "Urgently Seeking", "Immediate Start", that's not waffle, they mean it... they *really* mean it. And if you're the right fit, and you're ready to start immediately they'll see you as manna from heaven because those words indicate they are *desperate*.

**POINT THREE:** Sometimes RCs really overcomplicate things. Maybe it stems from the fact that a lot of jokes at their expense (usually unfairly) focus on them being a bit thick and arrogant, so they seek to use 'big words' to overcompensate. Who knows. All I do know is that you will occasionally read adverts where the RC has managed to be wordy and vague and has generally gone overboard: "Drawing on your wide ranging experience, your role will be to implement the strategic development of the dormant sectors of the target customer base for this demanding market leader." What on earth does that mean? Well; wide ranging experience is too vague to be of much use, market leader may be true or may be hyperbole, and the middle bit? You'd need to get the organisation selling to the customers they haven't sold to recently.

To read between the lines of their adverts:
- Dismiss clichés and hyperbole
- Take most descriptions with a pinch of salt
- Focus on what meat there is: What's the job? Who's the employer? What's the salary?
- Take note of the non-negotiables: if an advert says "Experienced XYZ" then experience IS required.
- "Urgently Seeking" means they're *desperate*.
- An advert with hardly any information given, and that ends "Contact Emily/James/Bob etc for more information"

usually means one of two things: either the RC is exceptionally lazy and hasn't penned an advert, or (more likely) they too are really desperate and time is of the essence so they've decided they don't have time to write an advert, and instead they've bunged that advert up and are currently ringing all their candidates in a frenzy.

**For extra info that's there if you look in the right places:**

   🖎   If the advert is on a jobsite, or a newspaper's job pages you will often be able to see the date the advert was posted. This will allow you to see how long they've been looking. Some agencies routinely update their adverts so they'll show up as new adverts to grab candidate's eyes and attention, which *can* prevent you checking how long the adverts been there. However the original posting date often still shows.

   🖎   Also, if on a jobsite, do a search to see all the jobs that agency has listed, you may see exactly the same job advert (or a very similar one) was posted over a month ago; so unless an identical job has come up (unlikely), they've been looking for a while. You'll sometimes find alternative ads for the same job, posted by a different RC at the same agency, or a different agency. It's worth looking at these various ads to see if you can glean any further information on the job, and to see if a certain RC's style appeals to you more than another's. That will help you decide who to contact.

   🖎   When you've found a job you're interested in (but not on the agency's site), then go to the agency's website to see if there is a more detailed advert there. RCs are often more loquacious on their own sites, in no small part because then they're not paying (directly) for the advertising space.

**As for agency websites?** Some larger, national or international agencies have professionals in to write or at least tweak their content. Other agencies supply their copy to the web designers and others write, and design and maintain their own sites. One thing they all have in common is that they want to convince candidates and clients that they're successful, professional, well respected, fast, efficient and effective. Another common denominator is their desire to make *you* as a candidate feel 'valued' and that 'your aspirations are understood'. And *another* common denominator? The opportunity taken for passing dig at the rest of their industry (usually cloaked as an admission that the recruitment industry has its flaws... and yet managing to extricate themselves from association with said flaws, and suggesting they're superior to their competitors). Consequently you'll see quite a few sites with spiel bearing more than a passing resemblance to this:

"Here at *BooglieWooglliePiggyJobs* we always remember that every candidate is a walking talking ambassador for us and our agency. It's all too common in recruitment for agencies to focus only on their clients. Of course we too are client driven, by which we mean we strive to source the best candidates for our enviable client base. However this is not at the expense of our candidates. Here at *BooglieWoogliePiggyJobs* our consultants aim to fully understand the aspirations of our candidates... yadda yadda yadda"

In a ideal world all RCs would live up to the spiel on their websites. But there again in an ideal world, I'd be a couple of inches taller, have legs up to my armpits, naturally blonde hair and be able to eat my bodyweight in sushi whilst maintaining supermodel proportions. Neither is going to happen in my lifetime, or yours. But then again when an A-list Hollywood star advertises a home hair dye kit, do you really imagine that every 5 to 6 weeks she's sat in her bathroom, watching a clock, with gloop on her head and the stink of hair colouring ingredients making her eyes water? Do you truly believe that's how she got her beachy sunkissed natural blonde look? No. She's simply selling a product. Now I know the ads don't say that she uses the dye, but I do think the implication is there, as she swishes her locks for the camera... Of course a agency website shouldn't be like that but the sentiment is not dissimilar, they want you to see the best sides of their agency. They're swishing their metaphorical locks like crazy because they want you to come in and register. So take some of their spiel with a pinch of salt.

♪ NOTE: Every now and then you see pieces in magazines and e-zines claiming to translate recruitment-speak (you know the sort of thing: "Flexible Hours = work 80 hours get paid for 40"). I know (hope) you'll think its crazy and unnecessary for me to point this out (and that you will forgive me for this moment of being 'Captain of Stating the Blooming Obvious'): such lists are funny, but of no practical use, so don't take them seriously.

## Chapter Seven

# THE SEVEN SECRET KEYS
# THAT'LL BRING THEM TO THEIR KNEES
(Ooooo that rhymes...

...of course it doesn't quite scan but hey, you can't have everything)

### Intelligence. Balance. Sincerity.
### Charisma. Control. Confidence. Communication.

If I was to reduce the whole business of handling your RC down to just seven words; those would be the words. A cute little acronym would have been sexier (and IBS (Irritable Bowel Bowel Syndrome) is probably not the choicest start), but this book isn't about prettying up concepts to be spouted out pointlessly, it's about the nuts and bolts of handling your RCs. Let's whizz through each of them, and their relevance in this context. We won't go over the top, as they're clearly not discrete topics; but rather, they're attributes and abilities that will continue to come up again and again throughout this book.

### INTELLIGENCE

I don't merely mean academic intelligence (A grades, distinctions and Firsts) and I don't mean straightforward IQ (although of course Double Firsts and an IQ of 164 do help). Rather I mean intelligence in terms of a quickness of thought, a savvy snappiness, a sharpness of mind, a quick sense of humour. You need to be sassy, spunky, sparky, smart ...in fact you need to display the kind of characteristics you hear referred to in American TV shows as 'smarts' or 'street smarts' (slang of course). Of course we all have days when we don't feel like the sharpest pencil in the box, but if you want to get the most out of your RC, you have to be on the ball. Try to always be one step ahead of them (trust me, in a lot of cases this really is not that difficult!). TIP: An obvious but useful technique is to think through *their possible responses* to any questions you're intending to ask in forthcoming discussions with them. Then you'll be able to think through how you want to ask the questions in the first place. Don't forget that how you ask questions very much effects the answers you receive.

### BALANCE

Not the high wire sort, the mental sort. Time and time again I'll recommend you should ideally do "XYZ" yet it will be followed with a "But not" or a "However don't...". *(See Page 113)* For example:

*Be engaging and affable, but not overly matey.*
*Be confident, but not cocky.*
*Be strong, but not pigheaded.*
*Be focussed, but not bolshy.*
*Be eloquent, but don't give the impression you have verbal diarrhoea.*

This isn't a cop out, it's simply because there are no absolute solutions. Let's face it, life would be a great deal easier if there were. But as there aren't, I try to flag up any areas where you need to really consider how to balance your approach. Metaphorically speaking I'm trying to provide you with a cracking toolbox, crammed full of tip top tools and gadgets, but you need to weigh up each situation, so you can decide which tool to use, how to use it and when to use it. Being able to take a balanced view and balancing your approach overall is an invaluable tool in RC handling.

You may be lucky and be one of those individuals who has always had a measured and balanced approach. Others are not, and have to work at it. The good news is that it's something you can actually develop, even if it's not something you're naturally prone towards. Its mostly down to thinking before you act, which is of course often referred to as opening your mind before opening your mouth. You need to get the knack of finding a happy medium. (Not Doris Stokes. (This by the way is a good example of a (dated) joke that most people don't even get and so should not be used in the presence of an RC or in any professional arena such as an interview.)) Balance is useful when you need to step back from a given situation to allow yourself time to consider. The degree to which you need to step back, and the time you can take varies.

## SINCERITY

As the old joke goes: "Show sincerity. Once you can fake that you've got it made." But seriously, be sincere. You need to impress upon your RC how important your search is to you, and how well researched and considered your search parameters are. Search parameters expressed by a flibbertigibbet are not going to carry the same weight with an RC as those expressed by someone sincere. Note: there's no need to go over the top, be sincere and be genuine but there's no need to get scarily intense and earnest (see there's that balance again). A decent dollop of sincerity in your dealings will do wonders for your credibility.

## CHARISMA

Rapport building is vital, a fact we have already established. It's human nature to help people you like, and RCs are certainly no different. So an easy way to boost your chances with them... get on with them. From that first email they receive from you, right through to the phone call to confirm that your contract for your new job is in the post, you need to be on the same team, and preferably on the same wavelength. Obviously you can't change another person's personality, and there are occasions when you simply cannot find a way to hit it off with someone, but on the whole don't give in. I'm not asking you to marry them, just to work with them to get a job! Be persistent, win them over with your charismatic charm. Be warm. Engage them. But be strong. Note: showing warmth and charisma is absolutely not the same as being 'nice'. (I admit I have an aversion to the word 'nice', it's so nondescript. So wet.) Anyway, all I'm saying is that there's no need to over egg the pudding, and I am certainly not suggesting you should be 'nice', or even worse gushy. (After all that can make you appear weak, and in turn can (in fact almost certainly will) result in your RC taking advantage of you. An example: they've double booked and need to shift around one of two interview times at the last minute, do they shift the sweet nice candidate who won't complain, or the strong, charismatic candidate? It's a  no brainer isn't it?)

So, when dealing with your RC be charismatic, be charming, be affable,  but be firm. Be the best version of yourself you can possibly be, because  your RC is your own personal PR man, and can, if they are so inclined, move mountains on your behalf.

## CONTROL

Fact is, the RCs like to think that they are in control, as we've already established in Chapter 5. Of course ideally they like to be in control but, as I'm sure you're well aware, *thinking* you're in control vs actually *being* in control are not quite the same thing. And that my friend is precisely where your intelligence, confidence, charisma et al comes into play.  You have to 'box clever', let them *think* they're in control and they're happy, and all along you're actually the one in control... and so you're happy. Some people feel very strongly averse to such approaches, and describe them as power games. Maybe it is, but I don't think so; a mind game maybe, but not a power game. At the end of the day it's in your best interests to get the very best performance out of your RC,  because that's the only way you can use them to secure the interviews, jobs, salaries and packages you deserve. And if it takes a little game playing, then so be it.

Being in control isn't about being bossy. It isn't about shouting. It's much subtler than that. Do you remember a childhood story about the wind, the sun, an old man and a winter coat? Ring any bells? It's one of those moral stories grown-ups used to tell you when you were a little squirt, an Aesop's Fable I believe. Yes? No? OK, well just bear with me.

---

**The Wind and the Sun**

The North Wind boasted of great strength. The Sun argued that there was greater power in his gentler approach.

"We shall have a contest," said the Sun.

Far below travelled a man wearing a big, thick, warm winter coat.

"As a test of strength," said the Sun, "Let us see which of us can take the coat off of that man."

"It will be quite simple for me to force him to remove his coat," bragged the Wind. The Wind blew so hard, the birds clung to the trees. The world was filled with dust and leaves. But the harder the Wind blew down the road, the tighter the shivering man clung to his coat. Then, the Sun came out from behind a cloud. The Sun warmed the air and the frosty ground. The man on the road unbuttoned his coat. The Sun grew slowly brighter and brighter. Soon the man felt so hot, he took off his coat and sat down in a shady spot.

"How did you do that?" said the flabbergasted Wind.

"It was easy," said the Sun, "So na-na-na-na-naaaaaaaaaaaa"

*(OK Apologies... I may have just changed the last line very slightly...)*

---

Now you're a smart cookie (we've established that) so I'm pretty sure you can see where I'm going with this but I'll spell it out just in case you're having a blonde day (I have them all the time).

So here goes Take 2... the edits required for Herbie's Fable:

**The Windy Candidate and the Sunny Candidate**

• Let's make the old man a Recruitment Consultant.

• His big smelly old coat is a cracking job.

• The Wind is a weary candidate who has had it up to their eyeballs with RCs not returning their calls, not fulfilling their promises and generally fannying around.

• The Sun is You. And *You* are intelligent, subtle, clever and if needs be you have a downright connivingly pleasant approach. Yep, you're the approachable, confident, can-do candidate who

wants to do everything you can to make that RC's life easier.
*So, here's (another) no brainer for you: who gets the coat/job?*
*Exactly. YOU do. The Sunny Candidate.*
**THE LESSON: It ain't what you do, it's the way that you do it.**

## CONFIDENCE

I appreciate that if you're naturally shy, you may think it's absurd for me to suggest you have to be confident, that *'you either are you aren't'*. Preparation is a huge help here. If you're not naturally confident, then by having fully researched all your points, you can have confidence in the views you're expressing, and in turn you'll give off an aura of confidence in yourself.  Confidence (but not arrogance) is an attractive quality that will inspire your RC to have confidence in you and in your abilities. After all if you don't think you're good enough, why should they? If you need encouragement or reassurance; remember that a huge proportion of the people you meet who *you* think are confident, are just the same as you. They've just learned how to give the impression they've got balls of steel, whilst inside they're as nervous as a turkey in December.

## COMMUNICATION

♪ IRONIC NOTE: One of the principle complaints from candidates is that RCs don't return their calls, and that their communication is lousy. Do you know what one of RC's principle complaints is about candidates...? Yep, you've guessed it: lousy communication.

Have you ever been in charge of a baby or a puppy that won't stop crying, yapping or baby-barking? Did you feel frustrated? After all they'd been fed and watered, there were no poop issues (clean up or nappy changing), they'd slept for hours so couldn't be tired, you'd hugged them, you'd left them alone, and yet still they wailed? Did you wish they could talk so you knew what the heck was going on? Well... don't be a yapping puppy or wailing baby. Communicate with your RC and let them know what's going on at all times. Got to change an interview time last minute? Make the damned call. Tell them as soon as you know. Putting off making the call doesn't make it any easier.  Don't pussy foot or filibuster, just be professional, clear, concise and consistent at all times. In short, maintain a standard of communication with your RC that you would wish them to maintain with you, and you'll have a solid foundation upon which to handle them masterfully.

# Chapter Eight

# "I WANT THAT ONE"

# HOW TO CHOOSE YOUR RECRUITMENT CONSULTANT

## THE 4 STAGE TECHNIQUE

**1) THE GENESIS:** You decide you're looking for a (new) role & you establish your search parameters.

**2) PLAN OF ATTACK:** You consider your options and after weighing up the pros and cons of the different methods you acknowledge (even if reluctantly) the benefits of RCs.

**3) SHORT LIST:** You identify and familiarise yourself with the agencies who work in the industries, locations and levels in which you're interested. Researching relentlessly you trawl the internet, you pick brains, you eavesdrop on tube conversations about wonderful consultants, and you assess which agencies, and where possible which specific consultants you believe tick most of your boxes. You create a short list.

**5) THE HIT LIST:** You hone your list, you fine tune it... you tweak and twiddle it, you watch the job lists on agencies' websites like a hawk... until finally you have a list of the RCs you are confident will do the best job possible for you.

## THE ALTERNATIVE 1 STAGE TECHNIQUE

**1) HIT & MISS:** See an advert you find half tempting, or call an agency whose pop up advert happened across your screen and phone them. Keep your fingers crossed & be prepared for the fact that you've made the next stage of the handling process more difficult for yourself as you are now dealing with an unknown quantity. You've risked ending up with a disinterested consultant who even your dog could have warned you was useless numpty.

I think it's fair to say that if at this stage I was to ask you which is the better technique, you'd go for the first. However in real life we both know that plenty of candidates opt for the second. Obviously the first is a more thorough approach, and the second seems much easier. The first one is rather time consuming and boring. It smacks of being the sort of goody two shoes who doesn't eat carbs after 6pm, or who always finishes their course of antibiotics. I'm not going to lie to you, it isn't a laugh a minute project, but (as clichéd as this may sound) every second spent in research at the beginning will reap dividends and stop you wasting days and weeks with useless RCs further down the line.

♪ NOTE: Of course, when time is of the essence, your research may by necessity be somewhat more truncated than is ideal. But do still push yourself to invest any spare moments you have to gather as much information as much as you possibly can.

## HOW TO FIND RCs

I was tempted to say leave no stone unturned, but that may (albeit it metaphorically) suggest all Recruitment Consultants live under rocks, and we've already established we're trying not to make RCs the butt of jokes and jibes (though I'll admit a wry smile has tiptoed across my face).

Your obvious options are online, in print and by word of mouth or personal recommendation. (This list is *obviously* not exhaustive.)

### 1) Online:

🖥 An obvious one, being as (according to industry surveys) roughly 80% of agencies advertise their jobs online.

🖥 Most jobsites have sections devoted to thumbnail adverts (or simple lists of text links) for agencies that advertise or post jobs on their site. TIP: Don't just look at the obvious, ie adverts and lists of agencies. Also have a look through some of the RC written articles or blogs on various jobsites, it's often worth reading these and seeing if you like their style and sense of humour as it's another way of spotting an RC with whom you may gel or click or work well!

🖥 Directories: Yellow Pages online, BT Online Phone Book (searching by Business Type), online agency directories, industry specific websites with pages devoted to careers will often have lists of agencies who specialise in your field.

🖥 Google it! (Or any other search engine of course.) Using keywords, you can search for agencies relevant to your chosen location, industry sector, specialism etc.

🖥 Print presence online: Newspapers and Magazines often have job sections of their websites (indeed some are well respected jobsites in their own right independent of the print item). Agencies often advertise on these and links to the agencies site are usually provided. There's frequently online content provided by RCs too, in the shape of articles and 'Top Ten Tips' etc. Again it's worth reading these to see if this is someone you think is on your wavelength.

**TIP:** when an agency's website address is not given but a contact email is (to send in your CV), then it's usually very simple to work out the address of the agency website. And, yes I do appreciate this may seem obvious to some of you, but you'd be surprised how many people don't see this as obvious! But to return to the point, if for example, if an advert gave the contact as:

herbie@shortstackpublishing.com

it would be a fair guess that the website would be:

www.shortstackpublishing.com

Of course this isn't foolproof, sometimes the website address is totally different, or in some cases you'll find that the agency doesn't even have a website. (♪ NOTE: as a general rule of thumb that isn't a very good sign; decent agencies want and need an online presence.)

## 2) Print:

📖 Advertisements in Newspapers & Magazines: National press, local press, industry specific press.

📖 Editorial: often RCs will write articles in the press to offer insight and/or educate the reader of course (though most would readily admit that the associated raising of their profile is a useful by-product). Again (as stated above) read these to see if you like the style and content, and glean clues as to whether or not the author is an RC you'd like to contact.

📖 There are articles written from time to time about certain agencies winning contracts to be the sole provider of recruitment services for a large company. If it's a company you want to work for... that's obviously pretty useful information. On the whole though organisations who use RCs tend to have PSLs (Preferred Supplier Lists) ie a shortlist of agencies they use, and an agency being added or removed from such a list is hardly headline news and so will not usually attract column inches.

### 3) Word of Mouth / Personal Recommendation:

🎤 Friends, family, colleagues, friends of friends, past colleagues, picking the brains of people within your chosen industry, social one off conversations (for example I know of candidates who have been at drinks parties when contacting me was recommended to them by people they'd basically only just met) (I found this flattering, but perplexing. After all was the small talk was running so so dry that the RC recommendation route was being furrowed?!)

🎤 A note of caution: it never fails to amaze me how much weight is given to Word of Mouth recommendations. Obviously, they are useful (they can be incomparably useful), and so serve a purpose. But remember they have their place along with the other methods, and shouldn't be relied upon in isolation. You should weight them appropriately, so if for example the recommendation came from someone you trust wholeheartedly and who knows and understands both your personality and also your career goals, that's a heavy weight recommendation. A second or third hand recommendation from someone you wouldn't trust with your shopping list is rather more lightweight: not to be dismissed, but certainly requires further research before you act on it.

🎤 To maximise the use of personal recommendations you need to expand on the initial information given (usually just a name). So let's do that...

## GETTING THE MOST OUT OF THOSE PERSONAL OR WORD OF MOUTH RECOMMENDATIONS:

OK, so we've established that this only works really really well if the recommendation comes from someone you trust and who knows you well enough to recognise who you could work with successfully. Whomever it comes from though, if the person giving the recommendation is a good enough friend or associate or acquaintance to have taken the time and trouble to recommend an RC then I'd suggest you ask some of the following questions (or variations on them) to ascertain the strength and appropriateness of the recommendation. You don't have to make the person feel like they're being interrogated in The Spanish Inquisition (...no one expects that...) but you can simply say something along these lines: *"I really appreciate your recommendation. As you've*

*been kind enough to make it, do you mind if I just pick your brains a little further?"*
Which will usually either get a simple *"Yes"* response, or a self deprecating one like *"Pick away... there isn't much to pick at... <insert their laughter at their own witticism>"*

**1) What or who are they actually recommending?**
Are they recommending an agency in general or a specific consultant within that agency? If they are recommending a specific RC; who is that RC (not just a name). For example in a small agency it's a big help to know if the recommended RC is actually the owner of the agency, or in a larger agency if the RC is a director etc.

♪ **NOTE:** Often the most valuable recommendations are for specific RCs rather than just generally for an agency. Within some agencies the RCs can prove to be a real mixed bag. Yet, it's fair to say that in a decent proportion of agencies the RCs are arguably all of a similar calibre (of course that may be a very high calibre ... or they may all be a truly dire bunch of eejits.) Generally speaking good, well respected agencies have good RCs (that's how the agency has built a good reputation after all); the flip side being agencies with a bad reputation usually have bad RCs (again, it's how they've got their reputation.) There can however be one off lousy RCs in good agencies, ones who've slipped through the net, and vice versa (with one off *good* RCs in lousy agencies). In both circumstances the one off RC is a fish out of water, and consequently doesn't usually last, or hang about for long.

**2) Is the recommendation based on first hand experience of the agency or RC?** Because if what you are actually getting is second or third hand you need to know the original source to assess the weight of the recommendation. For example is the source their sister who was placed in a great job last week? Or is it a friend of a friend who mentioned something in passing about them having nice offices.

**3) What is it that makes the RC or agency in question stand out in their opinion? What's so special about it/them?** Great jobs? Good client list? Great reputation?

Nice people? Great location? Snazzy offices? Delicious coffee and fresh donuts? (You can see certain points should carry more weight than others... I mean fresh donuts aren't to be dismissed lightly... ...weak & obvious joke, my apologies.)

**4) How recently has the person dealt with the RC or agency?** If they haven't dealt with them recently the RC may not even still be there. (The industry has a pretty high rate of staff turnover.) Also important because memories of how an agency or RC performed can be effected by the passage of time, and muddled with other experiences.

**5) Were they dealing as a candidate or as a client?** Obviously makes a difference to know in what capacity they were working with the agency or RC.

**6) Have they got a long-standing relationship with the agency or RC? How long have they had dealings with them?** Generally, the longer the relationship the greater the weight you can give the recommendation. This is because you can assume it's based on a long-standing, ongoing and successful relationship (even if a currently dormant one). We're working on the assumption too, that obviously if the relationship came to a messy conclusion they wouldn't be giving you a positive recommendation now (not unless you've really upset them at some point).

**7) How would they describe the agency/RC?** Ethos? Personality? Size of agency? Operating methods? Efficiency? No matter how well the person giving the recommendation knows you (or thinks they do) it's important to get some idea of whether or not *you* like the sound of the RC or agency.

**8) Any weaknesses worth knowing up front?  Are there any relevant issues they wish they'd known and with the benefit of hindsight can share with you?** Even the most admired RCs and agencies have a few flaws, and it's really useful if you know those up front. It's always great to be able to learn lessons from your own experiences and mistakes, but  if you can learn from other people's too that's a real bonus.

**9) Has the RC/agency ever put them forward for a job? How did it go? Did they get the job? Were they properly briefed prior to the job interview? How**

**long was it between them registering and the first job interview?** Similarly to #7 above, if you can get some idea of the RC's or agency's performance and processes you can judge whether they are up to your standards. Remember, your standards and expectations may be entirely different to those of the person giving you the recommendation.

**10) If they're recommending a specific RC, are there any other RCs in the same agency that they're familiar with and would recommend as a second choice or alternative?** Having a back up name is useful in case the first choice RC is no longer there.

**11) Are there any skeletons in the cupboard that you should know up front? eg Did the relationship with the RC come to an awkward end for some reason?** Did the person making the recommendation let them down and not turn up for an interview and then go quiet? Did they accept a job and then leave it quickly for some reason (some reason that had nothing to do with the RC or the new employer eg last minute relocation).

**12) Would it be OK if you mentioned their name when you contact the agency/RC?** It's useful to be able to say 'So-and-so recommended me'. Especially if 'So-and-so' is or was a top notch candidate or excellent client. The RC is likely to automatically associate you with them, which is a benefit to you. It's so much better than going in cold. Also, even if they haven't answered truthfully to #11 above (if for example they're embarrassed), then at least if you ask them if you can use their name, they'll probably say no, which means you'll be prevented from ending up being associated with someone who has left a negative impression. (Tip: (unless the person giving the recommendation is someone you know really well), then if they say they'd rather you didn't use their name but then don't offer any explanation as to why, just bite your tongue and sit on your curiosity or you're likely to create a very awkward silence, and you don't really *need* to know now do you?)

**Questions to ask yourself** to help you rate the person's recommendation:

**1)** Is this someone you know well? Do you trust them?

**2)** Is this someone who knows you well enough to know who you would or would not get on with or gel with?

**3)** Is this person a good judge of character?

**4)** Does this person know and understand the sort of job you are looking for in your search?

**5)** Also, it's sometimes worth asking yourself why the person is making the recommendation. Is the RC a mate of theirs so they're biased with no real knowledge of the RC's professional abilities? Are they just trying to sound knowledgeable and helpful to impress the people standing nearby? Do they think they know everything about everything and this is no different...

💣**Warning:** remember sometimes people make exceptionally negative comments and even offer warnings about certain RCs or agencies, that they say you emphatically should NOT use. These may transpire to be bang on the money, or they may need to be taken with a pinch of salt, or just plain ignored. Just ask yourself, and the person making the remarks, all the  same questions as you'd ask about a positive recommendation. (Do you trust that person's judgement? Why are they saying what they're saying? Was the source of the problem in fact their own fault in whole or in part? How long ago did they use the RC or agency? etc.)

We all know that sometimes reputations earned aren't fair. (But often they are.) Just don't take anyone's word at face value. Once you've had a recommendation (or warning) do some research to assess it's validity. For example, if you've heard that an agency keeps lots of old advertisements on their website to make them look busy with cool jobs, then keep an eye on that site and see how often the jobs change (though bear in mind the jobs may just be taking a long time to fill). If you hear reports that agency has been doing something seriously questionable, or verging on the illegal, this may be an agency it's best to avoid (although you could choose to research the claims to your satisfaction first if you were so inclined). And of course as interesting as the gossip factor may be, don't repeat potentially slanderous remarks unless you're drawn to the idea of involvement in a defamation case.

## ASPECTS TO CONSIDER WHEN CREATING YOUR SHORT LIST:

**SIZE:** Do you want to work with a large agency or a small agency? Do you have a choice?

Logically a larger agency will have large database of clients, and will also have more jobs on their books (Great!). The flip side of this is that they may have a larger pool of candidates to draw on to fill those roles, meaning you don't get put forward for as many roles and you *may* just become a number (Not great!).   Smaller agencies often promote themselves as offering you a more focussed, personal and relationship based service (Great!). They may have fewer jobs on their books, and a smaller database of clients.

Of course some industry sectors or fields are so specific that you have to work with a certain niche agency or two, thus removing the need for you to make a judgement call.

**HOW MANY OFFICES?** Do you want work with a large agency with offices all over the place? Could this be of help to you in your search, or isn't it relevant to you?

**RATIO:** How much attention do you feel you need? What sort of ratio (of candidates to jobs) would you anticipate? How many jobs would you expect the consultant to be handling? And how many candidates? Gathering real figures is tricky without either simply asking an RC directly, or having insider knowledge. (Although occasionally some agencies boast of the ratio on their websites, when trying to drive home the personal care and attention they give.)

**AVAILABILITY & FLEXIBILITY:** How easy is it for you to get to meeting in standard office hours? Is the agency's (or RC's) availability and flexibility an important factor for you? What office hours would you expect? What degree of flexibility? Do you need the option of an RC meeting you outside standard hours (eg if you simply can't get away from your desk in your current job during the day)?

**ACTIVE MARKETING:** Are you looking for an agency that actively markets candidates? Would you like or expect them to approach potential employers (who are not currently their clients) on your behalf?

**LOCATION:** Am not meaning whether an agency is in the

right city or town(!) am assuming that if you're looking for work in London UK you've made sure that you are looking at  agencies in London  UK (and not London Ontario, Arkansas, Ohio, Belize or Limpopo). Rather is their location appropriate for the roles you're looking for; eg in London generally speaking city agencies have a good proportion of city jobs, although Mayfair or West End agencies often have hedge fund, private banking, private equity jobs too.

**AGE, EXPERIENCE & SPECIALISMS:** Do you want an agency with  a wealth of experience? Are you looking for a well established agency that's been around for years? Do you want an agency with a specialist knowledge of certain sectors or a broader base? Are you happy to work with younger or even new agencies? Do you want an agency who regards your target area as a  key area for them?

We'll return to some of the above points, as many are the bases of questions and subjects for discussion with your RC in your first meeting. But before you can ask anyone questions in a meeting, you've got to identify who you actually want to meet! You need to generate your final shortlist so you can get on and in touch...

## DOING YOUR DUE DILIGENCE
## (CHECKING OUT SPECIFIC AGENCIES AND RCs FOR YOUR CONTACT HIT LIST)

Once you've got a basic short list of agencies and RCs, you obviously need to narrow it down. So work through your list and  investigate the points below.

In some cases you will realise very quickly that the agency is not for you. In which case strike it off your list and move on. (Obviously don't waste time and effort researching further points if you've already established an agency is a non-starter for you.)

**? Websites:** Do they have one? What's it like? Good design? Professionally produced? Done on the cheap with inadequate information? What impression do you get?

**? Jobs:** Are any of the jobs they appear to currently have on their books the sorts of roles that you're looking for? Are there many such jobs on the site?

**? Volume and turnover of jobs:** How many jobs are there on the site? How often do the jobs on the website appear to change?

**? Quality of clients:** does their website indicate the sorts of clients they deal with? Are there any specific clients listed (TIP: If there are no specific clients listed on the candidates pages, check out the pages aimed at potential clients. These often include testimonials from old and current clients to encourage new clients and in some cases build up the prestige of the agency.)

**? Clients' jobs:** Do the clients they claim to have on their books appear to be recruiting through them currently? For example  if an agency says they recruit for Advertising Agencies and list some as clients, do they have any advertising jobs right now? If not, it's still worth phoning to see if they expect to have such jobs coming in soon. (It may transpire that the clients no longer use them.)

**? Which RCs specialise in which areas?** Some agencies list the names and specialist areas of their RCs. Most don't. In many agencies RCs don't have formal specialist areas (though *informally* they often do). You can get a feel for the type and number of jobs handled by certain consultants by looking at 'their' adverts. How? You'll find RCs often use their initials as part of the reference code for the job, or their name or email is the contact.

**? Where do they advertise?** When looking at various publications in print and offline, and also looking at jobsites, have you seen their adverts? What sort of places do they advertise?

**? Reputation:** Have you heard anything about them reputation wise? (Note: how to assess others' opinions, recommendations or warnings, has been covered in great detail earlier in this chapter.)

**? Google:**  Google the agency. Google the specific RC. Don't give too much weight to any info you may find on Facebook or MySpace or any other social networking website or blog. (Though it suggests a certain unprofessional naivety if they are not aware of inappropriate content being easily accessible). This is an area we will return to shortly (Page 65).

**? Professional bodies:** Are they a member of a professional body? (eg: The Recruitment and Employment Confederation (REC)). Note: There's not a central licensing authority and not all agencies belong to an industry body. However those that do belong to one will adhere to its codes, standards and practices.

**Well done! With all that done, the God awful boring grunt work is out of the way. You've got your hit list so now let's start making contact...**

# Chapter Nine

# FIRST CONTACT

*You never get a second chance to make a first impression.*

Your first contact with your RC is crucial. As the hackneyed old expression goes: You never get a second chance to make a first impression. Of course psychologists, behaviourists, writers, lecturers, mothers, fathers and Old Uncle Tom Cobley and all will also warn you that strangers form an opinion of us within something between 3 and 17 seconds of interacting with us. This puts you under a lot of pressure to sell yourself almost instantly. The added difficulty you face with making a good impression on your RC, is that your first contact with them is unlikely to be in person. In all probability it'll be by email for example:

✉ an email sent directly to the RC, in response to an advert online or in print

✉ a speculative email, sent in the hope the agency or specific RC has appropriate roles on their books

✉ an email the RC will receive routed via a jobsite where you've responded to one of the RC's advertisements or where you've uploaded your CV to be found by RCs in CV searches.

You need to hook the RC with your words. The perceived wisdom is that as far as written first impressions go, you'll have up to 2 minutes to grab the RC's attention. Of course the RC will probably carry on reading after that time (unless they're inundated with CVs, or tired, or up to their eyes in admin), but your chance to make a great first impression has been greatly diminished if not obliterated, if they've had to *force* themselves to read on before they actually reach a point of interest. Remember though, if they *are* up to their eyeballs in work, (or they're doing a huge CV search on a jobsite and that's how they've found you) then you've *got* to capture their attention quickly or you're toast. In such circumstances they *won't* persevere, they'll just close the tab or window, hit the back button, or close the email. Ideally you need a hook, just as journalists do in newspapers in that oh-so-important first paragraph of an article. You've got to give them a reason to continue scanning through your CV and (where relevant) covering letter. So really dig to deep to think about why you're so well suited to the role and the organisation in the advert. Or if you're sending a speculative letter or posting your CV on a website with an optional general covering letter focus on what it is that makes you stand out. What's your USP? What can you bring to a role that's unique, or if not unique then still highly enticing?

With regard to  content, generally speaking: less is more. So go through both the letter and CV with a fine tooth comb to eliminate any unnecessary content. RCs don't like having to wade through lengthy letters full of extra words and phrases that fail to add anything meaningful or worthwhile. Use normal language, don't kid yourself that 'big words' impress, unless they're words you would naturally or normally use. Anything that reads as though you've swallowed a dictionary or thesaurus, or you're trying to impress, is a bad start. So make it all well constructed, clear, concise, compelling and convincing.

Remember that your covering letter and CV (whether sent to an RC directly or found by them in an online CV search) is just the first step.  I won't lie to you and claim that '*if you fall at this the first hurdle then you'll never get to the second step; meeting the RC face to face in interview*'. Because, you know what? That's poppycock and balderdash.  There's every chance you'll still get invited to interview with an RC, because some RCs are simply desperate for candidates, or (and sorry if this sounds harsh) some have lousy selection skills and don't filter applications effectively at all. Whatever the reason, if you do get invited to interview with an RC, but you haven't taken advantage of the opportunity to really impress with your CV and covering letter then you've already blown a chance to establish (or at least start to establish) the upper hand that's such a vital factor in handling your RC effectively.

## ON RECEIPT OF YOUR FIRST EMAIL
## WHAT'S GOING THROUGH YOUR RC's LITTLE HEAD?
**1.**  Ooooo look! An email. Ooo it's an applicant.
**2.**  What job are they applying for?
**3.**  Have they actually read the advert or is this just a general covering letter they send out to everyone?
**4.**  Are they already on our books?
**5.**  How do I contact them? Is there a phone number?
**6.**  It says the CV is attached. Is it?
**7.**  Can I open the attachment?  If I can, will it be a blank one?
**8.**  Oh good it's opened. Oh God its 7 pages.
**9.**  Oooo look its lunchtime.  I'll just go get a sandwich... and a coffee... and have a look at those shoes in that sale...

## THINGS THEY WON'T CONSCIOUSLY QUESTION BUT WILL ALMOST CERTAINLY NOTICE IF YOU'VE GOT THEM WRONG

**1.**  Is the body of the email addressed to the RC by name?

**2.**  Have you got the right agency? ie If you've referred to the agency in the email have you actually named the right one?

**3.**  Is the content of the email punctuated and spelt correctly?

♪ NOTE: The RC who is going over your spelling, grammar and punctuation so critically may well have flunked all their English language examinations since they were 10, but they'll still cast a critical (sometimes VERY critical eye) over your efforts. Unfair? Possibly. But is it what happens? Yes. That's life.

**4.**  A WOW factor. Yes it sounds obvious, but if you've got a WOW factor you *will* stand out. And please remember RCs will *not*\* dig around to unearth your WOW factor for you. You've got to give it to them on a plate. Inspire them, excite them... hook them!

\*Of course, *exceptional* RCs may do. But we can't risk relying on exceptional RCs, remember as a rule of thumb we're dealing with the average RC.

## THEY'VE READ THE EMAIL & OPENED THE ATTACHED CV. NOW WHAT ARE THEY THINKING?

**1.**  How long is this CV? What's the layout like? Is it logical?

**2.**  Do they have any relevant experience, qualifications or skills?

**3.**  What's this person like? What do they want?

**4.**  Do the dates make sense? Are there gaps in the chronology?

**5.**  Are there gaps in the skill sets and/or experience required for the job that they've applied for?

**6.**  Are they working now? If so what's their notice period?

**7.**  What's their current salary and/or most recent salary?

**8.**  Why are they leaving their current job? Are they being forced to leave their current job? If so why?

**9.**  Why did they leave previous jobs?

**10.** What is it they're looking for in their next job?

**11.** What are their expectations for the role? And for their salary?

**12.** Has their career progression been consistent? Are there any obvious blips I'll need to find out more about?

**13.** On the surface of it are they a possible candidate for the job they've expressed an interest in?

**14.** Have I got any additional/alternative jobs on my books that they'd be a possible candidate for?

**15.** Have any of my colleagues got any jobs they'd suit?

**16.** Do they strike me as a strong candidate and shall I invite them in for interview to register or not?

## THE THINGS THAT GET FORGOTTEN OR OVERLOOKED BY YOU... BUT NOT BY YOUR RC:

**1. Email address:** have a professional email address. Your pals may have found: heidihooters@... or studmuffin@... or vodkahound@... etc mightily amusing when you first thought of them, but they don't present a professional image. No, they're not an indication of your sense of fun and your individuality... they're actually just naff, tired and inappropriate in this context.

**2. Voicemail:** a very similar point to the previous one, but nevertheless comes up and again and again and thus is worth making. It's good to have a personalised voicemail message; it lets RCs know they've got through to the right number. But do NOT have a crazy, wacky or zany (even the words make you want to cringe don't they?) message which involves you impersonating Prince Charles, President Bush, Tony Blair etc or playing a favourite tune at eardrum perforating volumes (or in fact any volume for that matter). It's unprofessional.

**3. Facebook, MySpace, Bebo, blogs et al:** If you haven't already read of the horror stories of people losing jobs this way then I don't know where you've been, but be careful here. If you use a social networking site or have a blog, seriously consider about restricting access to non approved friends for the duration of your job search *if* (as is likely) there's content ('funny' comments from friends for example) that you wouldn't want an RC or future employer reading.

## YOUR FIRST CONTACT: 10 KEY POINTS

**1.** Be professional from the get-go.

**2.** Clearly fix your goals for each communication in your mind: your MUST inspire the recipient (your RC) to want to meet you.

**3.** Proof read everything again and again and again. If you can't communicate clearly and accurately with you RC in your first contact why should they even rate you as worth meeting?

**4.** Accuracy: correct addressee, spelling, title, gender and organisation. Proof read till your eyes ache.

**5.** Remember your Notebook of Success: fill in the data and keep it with you, it doesn't convince an RC of your fervent enthusiasm for a role if you can't even remember what it is you applied for when they phone you.

**6.** If it's a bad time to talk when your RC does call, then tell them straight away and agree whether *you'll* call *them* back (if so make sure you have their number!) or if *they'll* call *you* and at what time.

♪ NOTE: if circumstances dictate you'd find that conversation too awkward, then just don't answer (but accept you risk them not leaving a message and you missing your chance, remember the lousy RCs).

7.  Beware the scattergun approach: a late night application blitz that results in you emailing 10 different consultants about 10 different jobs at the same agency can just result in your emails being deleted (if the spam filter hasn't already taken care of that for them).  You'll dilute or at worst eradicate the impact of the one application that probably drew you to their site originally  ie the role that you wanted to be considered for in the first place.

**8.**  Attach your CV: OK so this does sound super obvious, but an amazingly high proportion of applicants fail to attach their CV despite claiming their 'CV is attached for consideration'.  It's not the end of the world, but it at best it slows down your application process and at worst suggests you have a sloppy lackadaisical approach.  ♪ NOTE: if an RC gets in touch to let you know that the CV wasn't attached don't get all defensive and give them that baloney line "Well I don't know why you didn't receive it I know I attached it".  It doesn't ring true and makes you sound a tad silly.

**9.**  Have a plain text version of your CV: some RCs systems will not accept emails with attachments so have a copy of your CV in plain text to cut and paste into their online forms if you have to.

**10.** Name your CV intelligently:  firstly resist the temptation to save your CV as the rather predictable 'CV.doc'.  Name it with your name eg:  HerbieHendersonCV.doc  it's one less thing for your RC to have to do (renaming it) and also reduces the risk of them losing it or confusing it with another. Secondly make sure you don't inadvertently send out a peculiar message with the name of the document.  Such as the message sent out by these genuine CV filenames sent to RCs: newCVmumsversion.doc (I know Mother's are allegedly always right, but do you think this RC was inspired to meet this 36 year old Mummy's boy?); oldCVwithout<*name of company that thanks to this document's title it was discovered on questioning them at interview that they had worked for albeit briefly, and left off the CV*>.doc; and finally  CV17.doc (That suggests a lot of edits don't you think?)

**So, assuming you've wowed them on paper, what next? Well, now it's on to wowing, and handling, face to face…**

# Chapter Ten

# FACE TO FACE:
# THE AESTHETICS & ADMIN OF
# YOUR FIRST MEETING WITH YOUR RC

*The secret of a good memory is attention, and attention to a*
*subject depends upon our interest in it. We rarely forget that*
*which has made a deep impression on our minds.*
**Tryon Edwards (1809 - 1894)**

OK. So we've already established you never get a second chance to make a first impression. However, the truth is that there's a caveat to that. In this context (the RC handling context) there are two 'first impressions': firstly there's the impression created by your initial written or spoken contact (which we've covered), but then there's the (arguably even *more* important) first visual contact. We want your RC to remember you, and remember you favourably. We want yours to be the name that pops into their head as soon as a great job comes in. So you need to make a serious impact.

By nature humans are very visual creatures; real and imagined images have been vital methods of communication for aeons. If you think about it, we're predisposed to highly developed visual sensitivity, from the ancient philosophers encouraging their pupils to draw and dramatise their ideas, to the Egyptians and their hieroglyphics, right through to the hundreds of commuters lined up next to each other training their brains with their Nintendo DS Lites. The point being? You need to have visual impact, you need to have a presence, you need to walk the walk, talk the talk and generally be the best possible version of You when you walk in their front door.

*Recruitment Consultants are like wet cement.*
*Whatever lands on them makes an impression.*
*So make yours a good one.*

**OK. So how do you make that great impression?**
This meeting or interview (either word fits the bill) is your opportunity to sell yourself. Your opportunity to inspire them. If this meeting interview goes well your RC will be enthusiastic about promoting you to potential employers. There are some seemingly obvious and mundane points to be made at this stage. Don't dismiss them because them seem so obvious, they're clearly

not as so few candidates take note of them. If they're basic and obvious to you that's great news, but they're included here because a (depressingly) significant number of candidates have repeatedly failed to give them due weight and consideration.

You need to think through the whole package: punctuality, preparation, presentation (clothes, hair, jewellery, make-up, shoes), paperwork, voice (keep it slow and not too quiet or too loud)... everything. So, as obvious as it sounds, sit down and think about all the things that count when making a great impression. And think about exactly what impression it is that you want to give. One of the biggest mistakes candidates make is to underestimate the importance of their dealings (and most significantly their *first* meeting) with their RC. People worry, and stress, and get themselves in knots over 'real interviews' by which they mean job interviews, but don't worry about their first meeting with their RC. And yet these same candidates would be getting a lot more interviews for better jobs if they had taken the time to prepare properly for this first RC encounter.

Some of these points do really come down to personal opinion. And without putting too finer point on it, opinions are like @r$£holes; everybody's got one, and sometimes they're full of ****. So if you disagree vehemently (for example on dresscode), then by all means go with your own judgement, but do so having read this and therefore having the benefit of knowing what the somewhat more conventional school of thought is... I want you to be able to make informed decisions, not rash ones.

**1) Do you know where you're going?** (Not only in life, but on the day... Do you know the full address?!) Plan your route and give yourself plenty of time to get to the interview. Make sure you have the full address, and how to access their specific office. What floor are they on? Is there a buzzer system at the entrance? Is there a security desk in reception that requires proof of ID before you're given a visitor's security pass? The importance of these points is twofold; firstly you don't want to give yourself silly aggravation and end up hot, sweaty and flustered before your interview. Secondly, if you're delayed because you get lost or you have trouble even getting into the building you'll have made a pretty poor impression on your RC before they've even laid eyes on you.

**2) Punctuality:** Don't be late. Tubes get stuck, buses break down, roads get traffic jams, but factor in the possibility of minor delays when calculating the time it's going to take to get there. It's better to be early than late, (though too early looks weird, so if you get to the front door an hour early, go grab a coffee somewhere).

In essence arriving late for an interview will always start you off on the wrong foot and arriving early will give you time to take in your surroundings and relax and prepare yourself.

If you're going for an interview in a lunch break from your current job, or are somehow taking time out in another way make sure you have allowed yourself enough time. If you're rushed and fretting about time pressures you won't perform at your best. Also if you've lied to your current boss and feigned a dental appointment etc, for God's sake only do it if you are comfortable with fibbing. I wouldn't personally recommend the fibbing route. You'd be better off taking a half day or finding a time your RC can meet with you in a late afternoon appointment. Candidates who have lied to employers often end up being nervy and panicky; worried they're going to be found out (and jeopardise their current job before even interviewing for a new one). The whole process can easily turn into a botched James Bond / Secret Squirrel escapade with the candidate acting like a defecting spy, all nervy and jumpy, looking over their shoulder and frequently checking their watch. (Also it's sod's law that you'll bump into someone you know and end up weaving an absurdly complicated web of lies). You don't want to have to be memorising weird fibs as Abraham Lincoln said *"No man has a good enough memory to be a successful liar."* Smart guy that Abraham Lincoln.

If you *are* unavoidably delayed, telephone the RC as soon as you realise you may be late. Ringing them 10 minutes *after* you were supposed to have arrived looks sloppy and inefficient.

♫ NOTE: Always try to get through to speak directly to your actual consultant if possible, that way you know your message has definitely reached them and has not been forgotten, altered or muddled en route to their desk.

**3) Dresscode:** Remember the last chapter? You've got between 3 and 17 seconds to make that first visual impression. Rightly or wrongly, how you're turned out does count. Be professional; dress appropriately. Generally speaking the rule is 'suited and booted', so wear a clean, well-fitting suit and smart shoes. If you're a boy wear a tie, if you're a girl wear make-up (though don't go over the top and trowel it on). (Yep, I know this may sound as if I'm letting down feminists who burnt their bras, but I'm giving you a general rule of thumb to help you make the best possible impression.) Have clean hair (the look should be neat and tidy rather than dragged through a hedge backwards), clean fingernails, (boys make sure your nails aren't too long, and girls the same (talons can look weird and unprofessional) also girls if you're wearing nail varnish make sure it's not chipped). Girls, if wearing tights or stockings take spares; ladders look ghastly. No overwhelming smells: avoid strong perfume, cologne or aftershave (and wear deodorant).

Beware the Orange & Yellow Tartan Suit Syndrome: if you can't bear the thought of 'conforming' and you regard your clothes as an expression of your individuality give some thought as to whether you're cut out for the job you are applying for. It may be that you know your wacky dress sense is perfect for the industry you want to work in, and you may well be right. However don't make that judgement based on how people who have worked in an industry for years, actually dress now. You're dressing to impress at an interview, not just for a normal day at work. People who are joining an organisation need to get their foot in the door before they wear certain items (in the case of the tartan suit mentioned above, let's face it, colleagues would need fair warning so they could bring sunglasses to work). If you want to wear something that makes a statement, then just accept that certain RCs (and further down the line, employers) will reject you out of hand. If that's a risk you're prepared to take because you're not prepared to 'compromise your individuality' then so be it, but at least make it a calculated risk, ie where you have actively elected to risk a negative outcome.

♪ Note: if your jewellery is unusual (eg huge silver skull rings) consider whether or not they look professional or appropriate. My advice? Remove nose studs, multiple earrings and outrageous jewellery. It may seem boring but it's only for an hour or so. It's not compromising your individuality, it's common sense. You wouldn't speak to your Grandmother over Christmas lunch using the same language you'd use talking to your mates at the pub would you? This is the same principle. (Note: if you *would* use the same language then you either have a very liberal grandmother, rather prudish mates, or maybe you just need to grow up a tad).

Having said all that, if there is a particular tie you wear that's very striking (though cartoon ties are a no-no) and you regard it as super lucky, or you have a pair of killer heels that give you an extra va-va-voom feeling of confidence then go for it. (That is: tie for guys, heels for girls... on the whole cross dressing at interviews is not recommended). You may think this sounds contradictory, but what I'm trying to communicate is not that you have to look like every other Tom, Dick and Harry, but simply that you don't need to look like a weirdo with no comprehension of the basic rules of professional dress. OK point made.

If you pick up a newspaper to read en route (useful to discuss any current affairs in small talk) but you pick up a tasteless tabloid, ditch it before you arrive. It's not the sort of thing you want sticking out from under your arm. Also don't buy a paper you don't read just to impress the RC eg a German broadsheet. (This is especially important if you don't speak the German, as you can bet your bottom dollar your RC will... fluently. It's called Sod's Law.)

**4) Names:** This may seem a tiny thing, but it can be so significant, and make such a difference. Make sure you remember the name of the RC you're meeting with, and for extra bonus points, if you've spoken with other RCs at the agency (possibly they've taken a message for you etc) remember their names too. (That way if you meet them you can say "Ah yes, David. Lovely to meet you, we spoke the other day..." etc. That person then feels valued, and you pay them a subtle compliment.

Of course the main person's name to remember at this point is your RC. If you forget their name, you look unprofessional and inefficient.   Even worse than just forgetting is the use of the immortal (yet frequently uttered) line

*"Sorry. I couldn't remember which one you were."*

This shows not only a basic lack of organisation (you don't  even know who you're meeting) but it also offends. You're suggesting the RC is one of many RCs you've lumped into the same box and between whom you frankly can't be arsed to differentiate.

So if you want to get off on a great footing with your RC? Remember them. Use your RC's name (and use it frequently) in conversation with them, by doing so you flatter them, you're saying that they've already made an impression on you. You give them a feeling of significance, of importance (...remember we're not adhering to the unhelpful social stereotype that RCs are all smug self important eejits already who couldn't feel more important if they tried). This isn't for their benefit in the long term, it's for yours. If they feel valued by you, you've made a positive impression on them and crucially you have their attention.

## 5) Paperwork:

### 🗐 Your CV

You've already sent them a copy of your CV, along with your covering letter (email) which has wowed them and whet their appetite. And that's why this interview is about to take place.

Nevertheless still take a couple of copies of your CV with you to the interview. Systems crash, cleaners knock over filing trays, RCs get sick (or resign, or get sacked) and leave their desks and systems in chaos... all sorts of things can go wrong that result in you arriving to find the RC you're meeting doesn't have your CV in front of them. In addition to taking a hardcopy (printed on good quality paper) take it on a disk (CD Rom) or some kind of portable drive (USB jump drive, your iPod (in which case take the USB cable to connect it), whatever works for you). That way if they *have* lost or mislaid it, you're ensuring they have in front of them and back on their system straight away.

♪ NOTE: If for some reason you promise to email the RC your CV after the interview (if you have to edit it, for example there's a typo you missed (though this really shouldn't ever happen) or maybe there's just something you've agreed to amend) then email it over at the earliest possible opportunity. Don't leave it for a few days. Firstly if you take a day or two to get around to it, you look inefficient; secondly you give the impression that your own job search isn't really that high in your priorities which in turn means that thirdly you'll lose impetus with your RC.

### 🗐 References

If you have copies of written references and they're good then by all means take copies with you. Don't take mediocre references with you (sounds obvious, but I've had candidates actively encourage me to look at references that I can hardly believe they've allowed to see the light of day and haven't thrust forcefully down a shredder, let alone shown to an RC). Some RCs will wish to speak to referees, or source written references as part of the full registration process. Others will only do this when you get a job offer. In some cases the RC merely passes on the referees' details for the client to follow up when you've received an offer.

At any rate make sure you have the basic contact info for the referees. Often when candidates arrive at an agency and are filling out a registration form that requires them to provide referees, you see them scratting around in their bags, or scrolling through their mobile phone's address book, or making frantic phone calls in hushed but urgent whispers asking for ideas for referees or contact details for ones they've thought of. This suggests a lack or foresight and a degree of inefficiency. It's just a matter of basic planning to make sure you have this information with you.

Standard contact information for referees includes: name, address, phone number, email address and the capacity in which they're being given as a referee eg academic referee, personal referee, previous or current employer, ex colleague etc. Make clear whether the addresses, numbers and emails are home or work ones.

♫ NOTE: With regard to your choice of referees. Always choose your referees wisely. Let them know you've given their details as your referees and give them a heads up that they are going to be (or are likely to be) contacted. It's a good idea to send your referees copies of your CV. They may indeed think you are the best thing since sliced bread (which is presumably why you've selected them to blow your trumpet) but that doesn't mean they can remember all the relevant who, what, why, whens, wheres and hows of your life. And frankly inconsistencies at this stage can be a drag. For example if your referee gets the name of your degree course wrong, or gets the year you started working for them wrong, it can cause unnecessary aggravation and can even begin to raise questions as to whether you've told the truth or not.

### 🗐 Passport &/or Proof of Right to Work in UK

UK agencies are legally required to check your ID and that you have the right to work in the UK. That's why most agencies ask to see your passport and take a copy of it (it provides proof of ID and proof of your right to work in the UK). If not a UK passport holder, you should be aware of your working rights, and whatever documentation you have (eg working visa) that will prove your right to work. This is what your RC needs to see (and photocopy).

### 🗐 Certificates

You can take copies of your degree certificate etc, if you think it's a good idea or necessary. But on the whole unless an RC has asked you to bring these documents you needn't stress over it. And if it later transpires that they do need to see them you can always take them in then. Of course having them with you in a file may be useful, and save the aggravation of a return trip further down the line, but don't over do it: there's no need to take *all* your certificates... if you go too far back in your education the RC will half be expecting you to pull out your first kindergarten finger painting at any moment.

### ✎ Photograph

Of the RCs I've spoken with opinion is split on this. Whilst generally it's agreed that photographs shouldn't feature on a normal CV (acting, modelling & performance arts CVs are obviously different) opinion is divided as to whether or not you should take a photo with you when you meet your RC. Personally I'd say it's worth it.

A lot of agencies will ask to photograph you during the interview. This photo is usually for their own records, to help them remember/ identify you.  Usually if they do this they won't want a hard copy photo from you, as they'll want a digital snap of their own to pop straight onto their system. However, digital cameras break and batteries fail to be charged, so yo may find the RC is flapping around trying to get a photo of you with failing equipment. In such cases the fact you have a photo with you (and  for extra brownie points maybe even a digital one on the drive with your CV?), is likely to be seen by the RC as a an absolute godsend.  An added bonus is that you have some control over the image then too. No doubt you'll choose a decent photo of yourself (no wacky holiday snaps, or best pal's stag/hen night snaps, obviously) whereas any photo the RC takes may well be badly lit with your eyes half closed and featuring a slight double chin... or maybe that's just me.

### ✐ Notepad and pen:

Take a notepad and pen with you, both to jot down any salient points discussed, and also so your RC *sees* you jotting down actions they've agreed to take etc.

### 6) Refresh Your Memory on the Contents of Your CV:

Make sure you can remember all the things you've listed on your CV and decide which points you want to emphasise in terms of qualifications, experience or work history etc.

### 7) The Advertisement You Responded to: A surprising number of RCs admitted to me that they do from time to time lose

track of which candidate is coming into to see them about which job. At this point you are no doubt shaking your head in disgust. However on the other hand a similar proportion of candidates I've spoken to admitted they'd been to interviews where they had no recollection about which specific job they'd applied for in the first place. So don't get on your high horse about it. Just be organised and take a copy of the advertisement with you. And to be extra efficient you could print off the exchange of emails between you and your RC so that you have, on hand, printed proof of the time of your interview and any requests made by them with regard to paperwork they wanted you to bring etc. This way you'll also have a full record of the progress of your application for your reference (the emails will show dates & times).

**8) The Questions You Expect Your RC to Ask:** Run through the questions you expect your RC to ask. Think through potential answers. Really give thought as to how to answer in such a way as to always be playing up your strengths and also giving them background on you that will stick in their minds. Practice with a friend if it helps, sometimes having the unpredictable element of another party to practice with can prove very useful. (After all it's really rather easy to interview yourself in your head and come out smelling of roses.)

There are lots of good books on the market that focus on nothing but how to answer interview questions. They're a good investment, and are worth reading thoroughly. (There may well be a brilliant 'How to Handle Interviews' in years to come, but as it would be a book in it's own right I'm not going to attempt to cover all the possible content here. We've got quite enough to cover.)

**9) Weak points? Are you prepared to explain them?** Have you given adequate thought to any weak and potentially awkward areas your RC may raise with you. Obvious examples include gaps in your CV's chronology (which RCs and employers tend to assume means a candidate has something to hide), poor grades, extensive job hopping etc. If in doubt ask a friend or family member to look over your CV and see if anything stands out (in a bad way). If there are any points or areas of concern in your working or academic history that concern *you,* there's a strong likelihood they'll concern a stranger (your RC). So think through how you'll address any questions or concerns they may raise.

**10) Loo, Face & Hanky Check:** Before you make your grand entrance find somewhere to have a pee if possible. Remember that a wise man pees when he can, and not when he has to (you don't want to wriggle and squirm your way through the interview with crossed legs). Blow your nose, and make sure you've got a clean handkerchief or tissues in your pocket or bag. (Runny or blocked noses that result in sniffing (even when you try to do it 'subtley') are icky). Also double check your face. RCs see more candidates than you'd believe with newsprint smudges, make up smears, lipstick on teeth, lipstick kiss marks, or food caked on their faces. So give yourself a final once over before you walk through the door.

## In Summary: Your 10 Point Pre RC Interview Checklist

**1)   Location:** Where you're going & how you're getting there.

**2)   Timing:** Have you calculated how long it'll take to get there? (Have you factored in minor delays?) If relevant, have you allowed enough time to be interviewed and still get back to work?

**3)   Dress:** Are you dressed appropriately?

**4)   Name:** Do you know the name of the RC you're meeting?

**5)   Paperwork & Notepad:** Have you got your CV (hard copy & USB drive)? References &/or referees details? Passport? Certificates? Photo? Notepad and pen?

**6)   CV:** Have you reminded yourself of the contents of your CV?

**7)   Advert:** Have you got a copy of the advert you responded to?

**8) Normal questions:** Have you run through the predictable questions you expect the RC to ask and prepared great answers?

**9) Tricky areas:** Have you given thought and prepared explanations relating to any weak areas in your CV?

**10) Pee Stop, Nose Blow & Face Check:** Just before your grand entrance try to have a last minute pee, clear your nasal passages & check your face!

**PS Turn off your mobile before you go inside.**

✿(NB: I know (hope?) this will seem obvious but, do NOT drink alcohol or take drugs before the interview. In fact, ideally try to avoid smoking or coffee just beforehand too. (Coffee and/or fag breath is a bad thing to be remembered for... as is BO, so while I'm stating the flipping obvious, if you're likely to get hot and sweaty make sure you've slathered on plenty of deodorant. You don't want to be remembered as 'The Stinky Candidate' (it *does* happen)).

## Chapter Eleven

# HEAD TO HEAD:
# THE BRAINS OF YOUR FIRST MEETING
# WITH YOUR RC

*"Your first appearance, he said to me, is the gauge by which*
*you will be measured; try to manage that you may go*
*beyond yourself in after times, but beware of ever*
*doing less." Jean Jacques Rousseau (1712 - 78)*

You may have felt (justifiably so) that the weight of the previous chapter was very much on what *you* have to do rather than what your RC should be doing. Well, in truth it was, but it *is* a vital part of handling your RC. *You* have to be the one in control (though they won't realise it), and in order to control them, you have to be 100% in control of yourself, your actions and your presentation.

As we've established, a large part of handling your RC successfully comes down to impressing upon them from the get-go just what a phenomenal candidate you are. But a difficulty you face in making a great first impression in an RC interview situation is that much of the standard advice cannot be applied. For example:

Standard advice: *The best way to make a positive first impression is to make the other person the centre of conversation.*

RC Reality: You only have a relatively short period of time in which to impress upon your RC just what an amazing candidate you are, so you can't make *them* the *centre* of the conversation, you have to talk about yourself. BUT do so conversationally, and engage the RC so they're genuinely chatting with you. This way they'll rate you far more highly than a candidate who talks about themselves without seeming to pause for breath. Remember 'telling isn't selling', if you simply jabber on about yourself, explaining why you're so great there's every chance your RC is going to tune out in less than 2 minutes. When talking about strengths and achievements provide illustrative examples. Don't just tell them you're creative; give them proof! If something crops up about your RC's own work history or holidays (or indeed anything) jot it down after you leave, it's amazing how impressed and flattered they'll be when you're able to make reference to such things in later conversations (especially as they'll have forgotten the conversation). However only do this in moderation or you may seem like a stalker.

Standard advice on first impressions that holds true with RCs:

🐾 Have a firm (but not too firm) handshake. If there's any danger of sweaty palms, dry them *before* you enter the office. A hasty rub across your backside prior to shaking hands just isn't nice. If (yuck) the RC has wet or sweaty palms try not to wince or be too obvious as you frantically try to wipe yours dry after shaking hands. (Using antibacterial wipes will also offend.)

🐾 Make and maintain steady eye contact. But don't stare.

🐾 Don't fiddle with hair, jewellery, buttons, cuffs... anything.

🐾 Don't fidget.

🐾 Be careful with humour. Quips may break the ice, but your idea of funny may not be theirs. You don't want to overstep boundaries and create awkwardness.

🐾 Speak so you're easily heard. Very your pitch to avoid dull monotone. Enunciate clearly and use hand movements and gestures naturally.

🐾 Steer clear of inappropriate topics. Your monster hangover, horrendous divorce or the fact you're premenstrual should be of no interest at all to your RC, and certainly have no place in the interview. Be professional. Think before you speak.

🐾 Smile. Remember you've already got their attention. Now you just have to hold onto it, and continue to whet their appetite so they want more.

OK so now it's time to turn our attention to your RC and some specific issues and topics you need to cover in the interview itself. This interview is not simply about projecting the image you want them to have of you, it's also about you assessing them and handling them. This interview will be the bedrock of your relationship with your RC so pay attention. First we're going to discuss (and then make use of) a human trait that researchers have labelled the rule of commitment.

**The rule of commitment** is this: once a person has verbally committed to an action it is more than 80% probable that they'll follow it through. There have been a number of experiments carried out over the years to prove the point, one recent one involved researchers posing as sunbathers on crowded beaches. The researchers would leave a towel and iPod on the beach whilst dipping into the sea for a swim, another researcher posing as a thief would then run up and 'steal' the iPod very obviously and very visibly. On average only 10% of nearby sunbathers reacted to this in any way (ie shouted after the thief or in a very few cases challenged the thief). However when the researchers asked nearby sunbathers to 'keep an eye on their stuff' (ie secured verbal commitment) before going for a swim between 80% and 90% of people challenged the thief in some cases actually tackling them and recovering the iPod.

How can you use this? In the course of ascertaining and agreeing a few basic facts in your conversation with your RC you'll get them to verbally commit to a number of actions. These will of course all be actions that *you* want them to commit to, but this way you will be handling them, and committing them to actions so subtly that they won't realise what's happening.

All of the points we're going to cover here are important, and shouldn't be overlooked. If you forget to cover the points in person during the interview it won't be as effective to try and cover these points over the phone later. (Though of course that is better than nothing.) Consequently it makes sense to take a notepad with you (with pre interview notes and questions), you can then refer to this during the interview and you can also jot down points.

When wishing to drive home a point (using your discretion of course, as to which occasions or points warrant it), make it clear that you are noting it down (as you're sat there in front of them). Note what has been agreed, and on issues of particular importance you should ask them to make a note of it too. Never bark orders at your RC though (sounds obvious I know but hear me out), you have to make them feel as though it's a request not an order, and if at all possible even make them think it's their idea. (This of course is a valuable technique in all walks of life, and is allegedly a key tenet of the success of those long and happy marriages... ...the ones where both sides have perfected the art of doing this to such a level that on occasions you just have to sit back at marvel at them.) But back to the point; your RC handling.

**1) The Brief: Your Search Parameters**
You need to make sure your RC knows *what you want*. And you need to make sure they know *why you want it*: you need to explain the research and consideration that has been given to establishing your parameters and goals. You don't want them thinking you've just plucked your goals out of thin air and fancy the sorts of roles you're describing merely on a whim.

Explain you goals in terms of:
- Part time or full time and temporary or permanent
- Salary range / minimum salary
- Industry/ies
- Location(s)
- Type of position and level
- Opportunities for career progression
- Package (eg are you used to gym, pension and more than the statutory holiday allowance? And is that the minimum you expect now?)
- Any further relevant points; for example hours/days? Flexibility in your working week? Or a contractual point, for example your existing employer may have (in your contract of employment) prohibited you from working for a competitor. Similarly there may be certain organisations you definitely do not wish to work for or with, in which case your RC needs to be made aware of those.

When communicating your brief to your RC, remember to listen to them too; make it a conversation. The benefits of this are three fold: firstly your RC will take on board your points far more effectively if you are engaged in a conversation, rather than simply listing demands to them. Secondly if they are a good RC you may actually learn something from them and pick up pointers. Thirdly by engaging in a conversation with them you're both building your relationship with them, and also allowing yourself an opportunity to assess them, their professionalism and their market knowledge.

During the course of this conversation make sure you communicate your well researched understanding of the current market, and explain how you have reached the conclusion(s) you've reached with regard to your value and prospects within that market. But, don't be obnoxious and don't be a know-it-all. That will just get up their noses, and may make them feel that if you're so darned clever then you can find your own flipping job... (Note: I'm not saying they *will* think that, just that they could do.)

Also, remember simply saying you 'need' to earn £30k to afford to live in your current flat, and maintain your current lifestyle does not illustrate why you believe someone would, and should, pay you £30k. You have to prove your worth and prove you have researched sufficiently to have confidence you can attain the package you want. But of course we know you can do that, because we covered all this in Chapter Three.

So, when communicating your brief to your RC, make sure that you're knowledgeable and *realistic*, that way you won't fall into the pigheaded and jobless trap!

Last but not least on this point, do listen to the information the RC volunteers, but also actively ask them for their opinion. Having explained what you are looking for and what you have looked into, ask them if they think there are any additional considerations or alternative possibilities you should be exploring. They may have some good ideas, and open to your eyes to a whole raft of opportunities that would interest you but which you didn't uncover in your research. Or they may be able to align your demands with a role in an industry you had ruled out, but one which you actually would consider in the right circumstances. This is where RCs truly can come into their own, as having met you they may immediately recognise opportunities for you that you could simply never have uncovered and thus considered. So talk to them, listen to them and pick their brains. Even if nothing exceptionally useful comes from it, you're illustrating that you are open minded enough to take on board new information and receive guidance from an <ahem> 'expert' and you are suggesting you value their input. This is always a winner in massaging an RC's ego or boosting their confidence, mood and general opinion of you. (Think RC ego: *"Ah ha. This candidate values my opinion... what utterly exquisite taste they have."*)

## 2) The Brief: Your Time frame
Your RC needs to know how soon you're intending to be in a new job. So depending on your circumstances you probably need to communicate one or more of the following:
- Notice (if employed): how long is your notice period? Have you given notice? If not when do you intend to do so?
- When are you due to finish your current course/degree/ training etc?
- When do you aim to be in a new position?
- Do you have any holidays booked? Give the RC the dates. It's phenomenally frustrating for RCs (and of course candidates, although the problem is self inflicted) to find a

new job is jeopardised because of a pre-booked holiday that the prospective new employer hasn't been made aware of early enough. Failing to alert your RC to pre-booked dates (weddings and long weekends away included) can result in the RC thinking of you as flaky and unreliable, when in fact you were just forgetful or shortsighted (although of course neither of those are desperately professional traits either and so should not be a part of the 'best version of yourself' impression you're setting out to give).

### 3) Communication:
### Your RC's Future Communication with You
Your successful handling of your RC relies on the relationship you build with them. And as is the case with all relationships, communication is vital.

Your RC may raise the subject of communication with regard to a specific action, for example:
*RC: I'll give you a call when I've heard back from the client*
...if so pick it up and run with it...
*You: Excellent, that would be great. Now when do you expect that will be?*
Don't allow your RC to fob you off
*RC: It's difficult to say they're such a busy department, but I'll call you as soon as I hear from them*
...and don't let them think they're pacifying or reassuring you. Remember you are in control...
*You: Oh I absolutely appreciate they must be very busy, but what time frame do you work to? How long do you leave it after forwarding CVs before requesting feedback?*

NB: You're implying they are efficient and are exercising some degree of control over their client (which they should be to an extent, but sadly often aren't.)

Remember you're the brains of the organisation (the organisation being 'Getting You a Great Job Inc'), you're handling the RC, never vice versa. If they don't raise the point then take the initiative and ask your RC how they usually communicate with candidates. Though don't allow that to end the conversation, you must swiftly make it clear how (what medium) and when (timing and frequency) *you* want them to communicate with you (ie you needn't accept how they *always* do it, if that doesn't work for you).

Before the interview you need to decide the 'Hows' and the 'Whens' of how you want your RC to communicate with you. Then during the interview make this clear to your RC. As already stated though, where possible do not issue instructions, make requests. And always always always elicit a verbal commitment from them.

## HOW: What medium do you want the RC to use?

***By email?*** Which address: home or work?

And a very simple rule: if you don't want them to email you at work (for reasons of tact and discretion e.g. they don't know you're looking for a new job), then don't give the RC your work email address in the first place.

You: *So how do you usually get in touch with candidates.*

RC: *Oh phone, email, carrier pigeon <insert laughter at own joke>*

You: *<polite smile at pseudo joke> Email is best for me, as there's no reception on my mobile phone in my current office. You have my email address don't you? It's on my CV. I've given you my hotmail address as obviously it wouldn't be very tactful to use my work address. So when you hear something from BooglieWooglliePiggy plc will you email me at my hotmail address?*

RC: *Yes*

You: *...just to confirm you will email my hotmail address?*

RC: *Yes I'll email your hotmail address.*

***By phone?*** In which case which phone? Your home phone, or do you have an unreliable flatmate/spouse/boyfriend/girlfriend who never passes on messages properly/if at all?  Your mobile phone? I've said it before but I'll say it again: for goodness sake make sure your answer phone message and your email address are professional or at the very least normal.  Your work phone? If you don't want them to contact you using your work number, then don't give them the number. However, being as they will know from your CV where you work, it may be worth emphasising this point by stating that under no circumstances are you to be telephoned at work.  I know of RCs who when frustrated at being unable to get hold of a candidate, have been known to telephone offices and ask to be put through; putting candidates in potentially awkward and embarrassing situations. If you want to prevent this happening to you; tell them that such actions would be unacceptable (though you may choose to tone down the language, it's your call.)

**WHEN: What time do you want your RC to contact you?**
☺ Be reasonable about this. They're busy too (at least they should be, after all for starters they should be working their butts off landing you interviews), so be realistic and accept that they can't be expected to call you at exactly 9am every day. So set sensible parameters and don't be ridiculously prescriptive.

☎ **Important note on their communication with you:** When (not 'if') you give RCs times and methods to contact you, make sure it is actually possible to contact you at those times by those methods. When you're in the process of looking for a job you're bound to have interviews etc that will crop up and mean you are out of circulation for brief periods of time, but just make sure you pick up your messages and respond to any from your RC as soon as it's feasible to do so.

You remember me mentioning earlier about both RCs and candidates complaining about poor communication from each other? Not answering calls, or responding to messages is one of the biggest causes for complaint on both sides, and is a trap  you can easily avoid falling into. So make sure you return their calls, respond to their emails and don't 'disappear'. If you feel they're bugging you, or pressurising you into something (for example an interview with an organisation you're not keen on) don't just ignore them.  If they're pestering you about jobs or organisations you're not interested in, (Note: it may be that you haven't briefed them properly, at any rate, see Chapter 17 on Troubleshooting); or if (God forbid) you've massively ballsed up an interview and feel embarrassed; or if you've got a job offer through another RC that you are considering... whatever the reason, don't ignore the phone and pretend you missed their calls. (*"Oh sorry the phone was in my pocket/bottom of my bag"* WHAT?!?! For 3 weeks?!?!? You see it just doesn't wash.) Be a grown up, bite the bullet and deal with it. It is always better to communicate so that all parties know where they stand. The quickest route to the circular file (or at the very least the bottom of an RC's candidate list) is to be a bad communicator, who appears to be impossible to get hold of.

✐ **Get it in writing:** This relates not only to written confirmation of points after the meeting, but also to making sure they've noted down your  important requests (well they're actually instructions, but as we've established if presented correctly they'll appear to be requests). So email them after the meeting to confirm everything you feel they should have noted down, but package it as a 'Thank you for meeting with me' email. With the points on record there's no excuse for them to claim later that they didn't know something that was in fact definitely discussed. Also, further down the line when they're contacting you to organise interviews for new roles, get written confirmation of: meeting times, addresses, names of interviewers, format of interview etc. Such confirmation (written) reduces the likelihood of slip ups. When someone has to write something down they are more inclined to double check it's accuracy than they are when just spouting off over the phone. (Most probably because that the written word is physical proof; it's not just a matter of arguing over who did or didn't say what.)

**How often do you want them to contact you?** It's also worth considering how often you want them to contact you, and discussing it with them. Some RCs prefer only to contact candidates when a potential job has appeared on the horizon. Others prefer to maintain a regular weekly or fortnightly contact, to keep track of how things are going. Depending on how quickly you want your job search to move, you need to decide if their standard modus operandi suits you. If you want regular contact, say so. If they say they'll 'contact you when something appropriate comes in', find out how soon they would expect that to be. Do not accept them fobbing you off with a 'joke' along the lines of, 'Ah well... how long is a piece of string?' Of course they cannot predict precisely when they will secure you an interview, but based on their knowledge of their jobs and the turnover of business in their agency they should have a pretty fair idea when they'll have something for you. Regular contact (usually weekly) really is the ideal.

Emphasise to the RC that you would rather they were frank (you mean 'truthful' but if you say truthful, you're kind of implying they would have been happy to lie... which will rub them up the wrong way). Enforce that you don't merely want to be put in some kind of holding pattern (see Page 116).

Explain that if you have a clear idea of the real situation then you will both be able to manage your whole job search more effectively, and won't be wasting each other's time. Also explain that you need them to be honest with you because if they don't think they can place you, it would help you greatly to know why. And that is 100%

true, not just a line. If an agent ever gives you the impression they won't be able to help you, you must establish why not. You may get some useful feedback, you may get some constructive criticism of your CV or interview techniques or some advice on how to play to your strengths more, both on paper and in person. Of course it may simply be that the RC doesn't have that many jobs that would suit your profile and your brief. Whatever the reason, if an RC thinks they'll have difficulty placing you, you absolutely need to know what the problem is.

**How often do you intend to contact them?**    Remember you're the brains of the organisation, and as such you will need to stay on top of everything, which is after all why you are working on How to Handle your RC in the first place.  There's no point in worrying at them like a terrier snapping at their heels (despite the fact that that image does make me think you'd be keeping them on their toes), but equally with most RCs there is an element of 'out of sight out of mind'. So a weekly call to keep yourself in the front of their thoughts is a good idea. Tell them that if you don't hear from them, they'll hear from you. Explain that you want to keep them updated on any developments at your end, and will be touching base to ascertain what's going on at their end. This is of course true, but it's also a gentle warning shot across the bows to confirm that you will be expecting them to have something to report to you, which will require them to work on placing you.

**What's the procedure when an appropriate new job comes in?** Do they phone you or email you when they have an appropriate new job in (or on the horizon)?  Will they always provide you with a job description (See Page 116)? (A job description is incredibly useful, so if an RC phoning you about a job doesn't offer to email you a copy, you should always ask them to email you one ASAP).

Ask them if they ever forward your details to clients without your knowledge.  The answer should be no. However some candidates are so keen to secure work that they merrily volunteer 'Oh you can send my CV out to whoever you think may be interested'. Whilst being so keen and having such enthusiasm is admirable in some ways, it does suggest a degree of desperation on the candidate's part, which in turn suggests that the candidate is not being discriminating enough.  It also puts the RC in the driving seat, and you're supposed to be there. There's no point in the RC busting a gut to get you an interview with an organisation it later transpires you're not interested in is there? So always make sure that they're going to contact you before forwarding your details to their clients. For your own sake you should keep track of everywhere you CV is being sent. This is the only way that you can keep on top of your job search and ensure you know what is going on at all times. For example you don't want the RC sending your CV to a company you had already decided to contact directly or that another RC has or had already contacted on your behalf. It potentially creates great confusion with regard to who did or didn't introduce you, which in turn gets horribly messy with commissions owed or not owed.

## 4) Your RC's Communications on Your Behalf:

☞ **Establish their procedure for putting you forward.**
Ask your RC how they put their candidates forward to their clients. Do they send your CV exactly as it is? (Almost unheard of as it's likely to have your direct contact details which could allow unscrupulous clients to attempt to circumnavigate the RC and their fee (which would of course be in breach of contract, but still occasionally happens)). Do they simply remove private information (contact details, referees' contact details etc) and top and tail the CV with their logo and contact details? (Quite common practice). Do they completely reformat the CV? (Common practice in larger agencies). Do they ever 'doctor' your CV (ie slightly adjust and tweak it, usually done well meaningly, but not generally a great idea (after all they could insert typos by mistake!), and completely and totally unprofessional if they would do this without telling you and getting your approval).

**?** Do they use your name? Some agencies do, some don't. Some larger agencies prefer to allocate a code to each of their candidates).

**?** Do they email *and* phone to put you forward? Do they provide synopses based on interviews and CVs? (Fairly commonplace). If they do create a synopsis, you're perfectly within your rights to ask them to forward you a copy. Bear in mind however that your RC may be reluctant to do this if they think you're going to tweak it and generally faff around wanting to edit it. Unless it is inaccurate or simply appalling, don't edit it when you see it; remember the synopsis doesn't have to be in your style as the client knows it is written by the RC and not you (which is as it should be - that after all is part of the RC's job.)

Seeing the synopsis is helpful so that you know both what the RC's impressions were of you, and also which of your strengths they have seen fit to play up to the client. This will of course prove useful if you're invited to interview by the client. Explain that these are the reasons you wish to see the synopsis (especially if the RC shows reluctance), and emphasise that you will not seek to edit it.

Ascertain whether or not they make a point of chatting with the client about you and their impressions of you on meeting you. This will provide you with some insight on the level of their relationship with the client, as well as giving you a clearer picture of their procedure. Find out how many candidates they typically put forward for a job. And how soon after putting forward candidates do they usually follow up, to get the client's response (decisions and feedback)?

### 🔋 Confidentiality & privacy:
It is worth checking how much of your information is entered on their database. How long is it retained on that database? Who has access to the database? What's the agency's policy on releasing your details to third parties?

♪ NOTE: so you don't sound paranoid try not to shoot all these question out like a machine gun. Just conversationally enquire about their confidentiality issues and if the RC asks what you mean then you have an opening to elaborate. For the avoidance of doubt, this is not an area where problems typically arise. RCs usually guard their candidate and client information like rabid  wolves, for fear that another RC may get hold of them. Nevertheless as a matter of common sense it doesn't hurt to both reassure yourself that your information is properly protected, and also alert your RC to the fact you'll be keeping an eye on them.

### 🕯 Your RCs Contacting your Referees: If you want your
RC to contact *you*, prior to contacting your referees, get them to agree to that. This is something that should ideally be confirmed in an exchange of emails. (Easily done by making reference to the agreement in the 'thank you for meeting with me' email you'll be sending them after your meeting.) If your referee is a current employer who doesn't know you're actively searching for a new role (obviously not the ideal situation), then for them to be

contacted would obviously alert them to your intention to leave. In this situation simply inform the RC that you will provide the contact details for that referee once you've handed in your notice and not before. (Do of course provide them with an alternative referee in the meantime, as they may be contractually committed to their clients to have sourced references on all candidates they forward.) By not providing the details for your current employer this pretty much eliminates the risk of contact being made.

## ⊘ Make All No Go Areas Crystal Clear

If there are any organisations you know most emphatically that you do NOT want to work for then tell your RC. Make it 100% clear that under no circumstances is your CV to be forwarded to Badoogies Inc or Numbnuts plc or Squidgybooger.com etc etc. Of course the RC may want to know why you feel this way (I'm already curious and I've never even met you…). You're under no obligation to tell them the nitty gritty details of 'why not', but it makes sense for you to have an answer ready to satiate them.

## ‖ You applied for a specific job. Questions to ask to establish to status quo and ascertain the next step:

The status quo:

‖ How long has the client been looking?

‖ Have they seen many candidates?

‖ If they have been looking for a while, why? Have there been recurring problems in the search? (A bad interviewer?

Difficult member of staff? Unrealistic person specification?)

Ascertain whether or not (having now met you) the RC is going to put you forward to the client. If they *are* putting you forward:

⠇⠕ When do they anticipate doing so?

⠇⠕ How many other candidates do they intend to put forward at the same time?

⠇⠕ How many candidates have they *already* put forward?

⠇⠕ Have any of the RC's candidates already been interviewed?

⠇⠕ Does the RC know how many people in total (including other agency's candidates) are going forward for these first round interviews? (If not, will they find out for you)?

⠇⠕ Is there any likelihood of the post ultimately being filled by the dreaded 'internal candidate'? (See Page 116).

⠇⠕ When should you expect the RC to let you know whether or not you have an interview?

ⓘ This is all covered in greater detail in Chapter Thirteen.

**FURTHER READING & ADVICE:**

There are a lot of great books on the market that cover interview techniques and interview questions. They're geared towards interviews with potential employers rather than RCs, but much of the advice they give applies just as well in RC interview situations if you apply a little common sense. The key difference between a run of the mill RC interview and one where you have successfully handled the RC is that you leave that interview in control:

- You know what you want your RC to do.
- You know whether or not they can do it.
- You've told them how you want it to happen (taking into account all the factors you have no control over ie the market at the time).

In conventional job interviews with potential employers, you're not in control (obviously) and you certainly aren't directing them. So when reading books specialising in interview techniques always temper the advice, and remind yourself that you're in control when with your RC. It comes down to power. Broadly speaking in a job interview the interviewer has a job that you want, and they have the power to give you that job. Whereas in an RC interview, the RC has a client with a job that you want, the RC can (if they so wish) pitch you to their client to get you an interview. That's the only source of their power. The RC does not have the power to give you that job.

**A FINAL THOUGHT:**

*"If you would stand well with a great mind, leave him with a favorable impression of yourself; if with a little mind, leave him with a favorable impression of himself."*

Samuel Taylor Coleridge (1772 - 1834)

Now, I'm not saying your RC is a great mind, nor am I saying they're a little mind; I'm just suggesting you hedge your bets and walk out of their offices leaving them with a favourable impression of yourself *and* a favourable impression of themselves.

# Chapter Twelve

# MAINTENANCE

It sounds so painfully obvious, but stay in touch. Don't rely on your RC to make the running. Of course your RC may be great at communicating, and keep you in the loop on all developments at all possible stages, just don't count on it. The earlier point regarding keeping your name and profile at the front of their minds is a vital one. It's not fair, but it's logical; you're more likely to get placed if your RC is thinking about you.

If one of your RCs secures you an interview let your other RCs know. This is both practical and motivational: the RC needs to know how your search is going, and it's also likely that they'll be motivated to get their fingers out and work extra hard to get you interviews too. After all they don't want to miss out on a potential commission, and the old adage about *'nothing succeeds like success'* holds water here too: if mentally your RC thinks of you as a desirable candidate that others want that'll really work to your advantage.

But be warned: no matter how desirable you wish to appear: making up interviews (past or future) is an appalling idea. You may get caught out, which leaves you branded as a liar or a fantasist (neither being desirable traits). Or you could find you've shot yourself in the foot: a serial interviewee who never quite seems to land the job? That's not a successful candidate; that's either an overly picky candidate or one with lousy interview skills and the odour of failure lingering about their person...

Keep your RC up to date with your thinking and your CV. A stunningly large proportion of candidates shift the focus of their search (and rewrite their CV to reflect this) and yet omit to mention it to their RCs.

Assuming you're keeping on top of your administration (including of course your Notebook of Success) you'll have records of which RCs you registered with at which agencies. As you update your CV (which of course you may do on graduation (obviously) or on completion of an internal training course, or simply because time has passed since the start of your search etc); send a copy to your RCs. Keep meticulous records, so you always know which version of your CV each RC has on their files. And after sending it to the

RCs, phone them to get confirmation that they have updated their records accordingly. Otherwise it's the sort of admin task they'll consign their 'to-do at some point' pile or list, never to see the light of day again.

Regular contact with your RC will not only keep them thinking about you, and searching for jobs for you, but will also help to develop your relationship with them and strengthen it. Each time you're in contact it should build on the previous time. If you leave it too long, you'll end up with awkward conversations and you'll lose the rapport you've worked hard to build.

As the relationship develops you may be tempted to joke and become increasingly informal, but remember the relationship is a professional one. Of course humour and joviality is an important part of rapport building and of maintaining your relationship with your RC. However not everyone's sense of humour is the same, so be selective. In exceptional circumstances long term friendships and personal relationships do develop, but before we find you a soul mate and/or a spouse shall we just concentrate on finding you a job?

Always keep your RC up to speed with all developments in your search. Close each communication with confirmation of when you will next be in touch, or when you expect to hear from them. If you find a job through another RC, or if you have a total change of heart, and decide to up sticks and go travelling for a year, or decide to train as an aromatherapist, or go back to Uni with the intention of becoming a psychiatrist they'll understand (hell they may even use your services). They'll be a lot less understanding though if they've been trying to contact you to no avail for yonks and you haven't returned their calls or emails. So stay in touch and keep them in the loop. If you change you mobile number, let them know. Switch your internet provider and your main email account, let them know. A last minute bargain trip to the Maldives may seem like less of a bargain if you miss out on your dream job because your RC assumed you'd cut all ties with them, rather than letting them know what they should do in your absence, and whether you'd have access to email.

It's like any other relationship in many ways, you have to work at it. (Just in this relationship you don't have to listen to them burble drivel when sloshed or put up with their hair in the plughole.)

# Chapter Thirteen

## PRE JOB INTERVIEW

**Congratulations! You've landed the interview!**
**Now what?** This is where you can really make your RC sing for
their supper. They will have insights you simply couldn't have.
And you need to milk all the information you can from them.

### 1) The Basics & Practicalities
All this information should be provided by your RC:
• The full address of the interview (including floor number
if appropriate), and do they have a map they can email you?
(Often, especially for tricky addresses, maps with detailed
directions are sent by the client to the RC).
• The full names, titles and job titles of the person/people
interviewing you.
• Who should you ask for on arrival?
• If you're not being interviewed by the person who will
ultimately be your superior/boss/line manger etc, then will you
have the opportunity to meet them at this stage?
• The format of the interview. For example: is it merely a face
to face question and answer session or is there some testing
involved?
• The time of the interview.
• The likely length of the interview.
• Any specific information regarding access to the building.
For example will security require proof of ID?
• Any quirks of the location, for example is the front door
unmarked with an unlabelled buzzer entry? (This happens...)
Whilst the RC may not know all this, they can enquire on your
behalf, or they may know first hand from visiting the premises
when they first landed the business.
• Get all of this in writing (email is, as always, fine). You want
to be confident you have all the information you need, and
you need to have it in writing for two main reasons. Firstly
as we've established RCs are more inclined to make sure
they're providing all the correct information when they have
to commit to putting it in writing. Secondly, should there be
a problem, and your RC gets the office or the time wrong you
can (if necessary) prove the fault was not with you. (Sorry to
say it, but RCs have been known to let the client believe the

candidate was at fault, in order to save face.) If you have it in writing this limits the likelihood of the RC trying to pull that one. However if the interview is rearranged (after the RC has mucked up) if you arrive, pull the email out and thrust it under the nose of your interviewer to 'prove' it wasn't your fault (that the previous interview didn't happen).... then you may look paranoid, slightly mental, or simply as though you are telling tales out of school. You could however make a passing reference to the 'unfortunate mistake' the RC made in the email they sent you, and thank the interviewer for not allowing the RC's error to prejudice them.

•  Confirm the job title. (You would obviously already know this before having been put forward, but double check all the info.)

•  Confirm the salary/package?    Is there any room for negotiation? Has the RC already revealed to the client what you are looking for in terms of salary? (This would be vital information for you to have ahead of time if any salary conversation cropped up in the interview.)

•  How soon does the client want the successful candidate to start the job?

•  If you haven't already seen it, ask the RC to forward you a copy of the job description. If they don't have a formal one, ask them if they can get you one from the client, or if that's not possible then ask them to draft an informal job description. (Some RCs may be reluctant to commit it to email, however you can cajole (some would say trick) them into doing this:

You: *Can you forward me a copy of the job description?*

RC: *I'm afraid the client hasn't provided one.*

You: *Well could you ask the client for one?*

RC: *There isn't a formal one. I can tell you what you need to know.*

(If this is the RC's response it's likely to be because (a) it's true(!) or (b) because they didn't get a formal one at the start and now don't want to seem a numbnut going back to the client saying they don't really know enough about the job to describe the role to their candidates.)

You: *Oh OK. That's great. So you know roughly what would be in job description?*

RC: *Oh yes absolutely.* (Won't want to lose face or look inefficient.)

You: *Fabulous, can you jot that down in an email for me then?*

RC: *Er, well I could just tell you now if you like. I mean that'd be quicker.* (Remember RCs often aren't keen to commit info to email if they aren't confident of the details.)

You: *I think it would be best to have it in an email. I can always call you if I have any questions.* (At the end of the day you should end up with something written and fairly accurate.)

## 2) Background on the organisation:

Some of this information can and should be provided by your RC and some of it can and should be unearthed by your own research and due diligence. It is not, on the whole, content that you should expecting your RC to spoon feed to you. It's your responsibilty to find out most of this and usually even the most cursory Google search will be a good start. Having said that if your research unearths nothing, you should get straight on the phone or email to pick the brains of your RC.

- Basic background info. Websites are first port of call. Does the organisation have a website? What's the address? Most organisations have websites nowadays, however in the cases of those that don't or who have little or no information on said websites (or have them password locked so the public can't access them) you'll need to get a little more creative. This may be as simple as ringing up and asking for a brochure or simply some information on the company. Or you may need to think outside the proverbial box, though asking your RC for more background is a good start (having explained there is no website, and so you're not asking because you're lazy).
- How many employees (ballpark is fine)?
- How many offices? Where's the head office?
- Has the organisation been in the news at all recently?
- Who are their competitors?
- Any big news stories involving them in recent years?
- Is the organisation part of a much larger group?
- Have they landed any major new business recently etc.

## 3) Get the skinny: the inside track on the interview, the interviewers and the job:

Some of these points are likely to have been covered in your conversations with your RC prior to getting the invitation to interview. However if the points *haven't* come up, now's your chance. Some of the points may be areas you'll want to raise in the job interview itself: for example you may elect to ask your interviewer why the post is being created, or why the previous incumbent is leaving (if your RC couldn't answer this point).

• How many other candidates did your RC eventually put forward for the job? And how many of them are going forward for interview?

• Are there other agencies working with the client on this job? Is your RC aware of how many of their candidates are going forward for interview? So overall does your RC know how many people are going forward for these first round interviews? (If not, will they find out for you?)

♪ Note: a decent RC should have already asked the client... but for whatever reason your RC may not have done.)

• Is there any likelihood of the post ultimately being filled by the dreaded 'internal candidate' (See Page 116).

• What's the organisation like in terms of style and spirit? The 'organisational culture' if you will.

• Has the organisation been trying to fill this post for a long time? If so why?

• Does the RC know why the previous incumbent left, or is leaving?

• If this is a new role, does the RC know why it is being created?

• Has the RC placed people within the organisation before? (Or have other RCs at the agency?) If so, what's their feedback on the place? Are they still there? Do they enjoy it? Have they been promoted? Have they left? (And if so then why?)

• In your RC's opinion are the interviewers actually good at interviewing? (An awful lot aren't terribly good.) What are the interviewers actually like? (Some organisations (for reasons that escape me) appear to entrust the interviewing process to individuals with the people skills of Hannibal Lecter with his fava beans ready and his chianti open).

• Has the organisation got any skeletons in the cupboard? This can be helpful in making sure you don't stumble into tricky areas by mistake during your interview. (For example: asking about the office culture, and whether or not it is a 'work hard play hard' environment when a couple of employees have just been arrested for supplying cocaine to other drunken revellers during a drunken office night out, *may* make the interviewer think you're a smart arse who is taking the mickey.)

• Are there any particular questions that seem to come up again and again at this organisation? I know of one organisation who always asked 'Would you be prepare to break the law for your employer?' and 'If I have a cricket bat and ball worth £125 and the bat is £100 more expensive than the ball, how much is the ball?' Both questions threw several candidates. (The cricket question seems simple in the cold light of day, but in fairness when it's emphasised that speed is of the essence it's not so easy. For the avoidance of doubt the answer is £12.50.) Point is, if you can get a heads up on any questions that's a big bonus.

## 4) What next?

This is an area you will probably cover in the interview with the prospective employer, but your RC should be able to give you a heads up.

•   Do they expect to be carrying out second interviews or will they be making a decision based solely on this first one? (Unusual, but it happens.)

•   How soon would the RC expect to hear from the client? And how long will they leave it before chasing them up if they haven't heard anything?

•   Does this client typically move quickly?

•   Are there any other jobs in the pipeline that the RC thinks may be of interest to you? (It's always useful to get an idea of your options; although RCs may give a somewhat guarded and not completely full (and truthful) answer at this point, as they will want you to be fired up with drive and enthusiasm for the interview that's already on the cards. This is to a point understandable, as a bird in the hand is worth two in the bush and all that.)

All the normal rules apply in terms of your preparation. You should know where you are going, how to get there, how long it will take, what to wear, think through all the likely interview questions (as I've said there are some excellent books on the market that go through interview questions and great answers, along with books focussing on what you should ask), it's all the standard stuff. (See Page 76 for the pre RC interview checklist).

Most importantly remember: you've landed the interview because you're You and the potential employer likes what they've seen and heard so far. So well done and good luck!

# Chapter Fourteen

# POST JOB INTERVIEW

**Phew. It's over. Cue a big sigh of relief.**
You'll be calling your RC shortly to give them post interview feedback, but first you need to catch your breath and think through where you stand. Don't switch your mobile on yet, as you need to compose your thoughts and don't want anyone (especially your RC) to phone your mobile and interrupt that process.

**Take a few moments to mull everything over.**
Find a good spot and give yourself a time to take stock of the last hour (or however long the interview took). Pull out your notepad and pen and jot down all the key points that came up, plus others that will have come to mind during the course of the interview:

🖋 Names: jot down the names (and job titles or roles, even if only approximately) of everyone you met, and also jot down a brief description of what they look like. It's amazing how after a few hours John merges into George, and how it's suddenly impossible to differentiate between Lucy and Natasha in your mind's eye. (In a job interview one December (one where I subsequently got offered and accepted the job) I became totally confused over the names of two other employees. I spent the whole Christmas hols and then embarrassingly the first few days at work having to think REALLY hard before I addressed either of them... and even then I got it wrong several times, and the worst part of it all? There were only 5 people in the office in total. It took me ages to get them straight in my head.)

🖋 Questions you had difficulty answering. That way if those questions come up again, you'll have knock out answers ready.

🖋 Any questions you wish you'd asked the interviewer(s).

🖋 Any concerns you have, now you've learnt a little more about the job and the organisation.

🖋 Any issues you'd like to discuss with your RC. These may for example be relating to the next stages of the process with the particular company where you were just interviewed. Or they may be issues that popped into your head during the interview, ie prompted by something the interviewer mentioned.

🖋 Anything else buzzing around your mind, be it incredibly

salient points, or simply shopping list items that have sprung to mind mid interview (though in fairness this may not happen to you, I only mention it because my little brain always seems to remind me of the urgent need for a loaf of bread, dog food and some washing up liquid at the most inopportune moments). You should do this so there is nothing cluttering your thoughts.

Having made your notes, give some thought as to how you feel about the interview overall, the people you met, the job itself, any huge plus points and any areas of concern. Questions to ask yourself would probably include the following:

**?** Do you feel the interview went well overall? Are there lessons you can learn to improve your interview technique?

**?** Did you think the interviewer was a good interviewer? Or did you get the impression they didn't really know what they were doing? If you have any concerns about the interviewer's abilities, this is something you should mention to your RC. It could unfairly prejudice the outcome of your interview. (Remember that whilst the person carrying out the first interview often isn't officially the final decision maker, they could prevent you making it through to the next round.)

**?** Was there an important point you wished you'd made that completely slipped your mind? Again tell your RC, they'll usually be able to communicate it on your behalf.

**?** Did you like the people you met? Did you like the office? Did you feel the job, the people and organisation were in keeping with what you were expecting?

**?** Are there people you'd like to meet before being confident this is the job for you? (Team members, managers etc).

**?** If they offered you a second interview would you want to take it?

**?** The big one: if they offered you the job would you take it?

**OK. Switch your mobile on,** get your notepad out, look over your notes. *Now* ring your RC. Give them feedback on the interview and ask your questions. Let the RC know your current thinking: are you still keen on this job. Finally make them commit to phoning you as soon as they get client feedback. Then give your brain a rest. Don't brood, just get on with your day. Well done!

# Chapter Fifteen

# RESULT: OFFER? SECOND INTERVIEW? REJECTION? SILENCE?

**After what seems like forever, finally your RC calls!**
The length of time between your interview and the client calling your RC with feedback depends on a number of factors. For example: how many other interviews still had to be carried out and how long they took; whether the interviewer was tied up with other work projects that took their attention away from the recruitment process; whether the interviewer had to go away on business, was ill or went on holiday; or even if they were simply having difficulty deciding which candidate(s) they'd like to see again.

Your RC should have alerted you to any potentially long wait (if it was predictable) but that doesn't make the waiting any easier. For the purposes of this chapter I'm assuming you want the job in question (because frankly if you don't then the result of your first interview is of very limited interest to you, in fact the only point of interest may be any feedback on your interview technique). And if you think this chapter is short please, do remember this book is about 'How to Handle Your RC' so despite the fact that this is an important stage in your job search, it is not an area of huge focus for this book. It's the getting to this stage, that will have involved the bulk of the RC handling you need to do.

**OFFER:** WOW! What can I say? You've clearly done everything right! You're the man or woman for the job; you've impressed them in person, on paper and they want you. Huge congratulations. Of course your RC has played a part in this too; probably not as big a part as they think (because it's in the nature of most RCs to enjoy revelling in the associated glory of having a successful candidate). All the time and effort you've put into preparing and performing at interview has paid off.

You needn't feel you have to rush into accepting this (or any) position. Most organisations won't expect you to accept or reject an offer immediately, though do bear in mind that some are a great deal more impatient than others. Your RC will be able to tell you whether or not the organisation in question is one of the impatient ones (on the whole they tend to be the ones who have their pick of great candidates, and so believe you should bite their arms off... and I guess you can sort of see where they're coming from, nevertheless I can't help but think it seems quite pompous and self important to be so convinced that you should be grateful they've honoured you with an offer).

If you're happy with the whole package that's on offer, and you're happy to accept, then of course go for it! Yelp with delight and allow your RC to share that moment of pure celebration and happiness with you. Announcing to a candidate that they've landed a job they really want is (I can personally testify) one of the absolute highlights of life as an RC.

However if you have another offer on the table, or you have certain points that require clarification before you feel you can accept, then just tell your RC straight away. But, do show some gratitude and happiness about the offer. Remember you don't know what's around the corner, and now is not the time to make your RC feel you're an ingrate.

Under no circumstances allow your RC to bulldoze you into accepting a job you don't want. Frankly they're foolish if they try to do so, as it will damage their reputation in the long run (let's face it, you're going to mention such behaviour to your contemporaries) and it'll undermine or even destroy your relationship with your RC. Also, for your information, if you leave within 10 weeks or 3 months (usually it's one or the other) the agency has to refund all or part of the fee for finding you. Which of course means that the RC either doesn't get commission on the placement or, (which seems in some ways even worse), they get it and then have to pay it back (it's worse as they've often already spent it...).

Of course you don't have to give your RC an immediate acceptance or rejection; but providing you've given it due consideration before you get the call you should be in a good position to give the RC a considered response. If you *do* want to accept the job, but would like to push for a better package than is currently on the table, your RC will be able to help. For a more detailed discussion of contract negotiation and acceptance head straight to the next chapter (Page 106). A couple of brief notes on this point though:

    ♪ Have you already discussed possible package with the client in the interview? Have you given them impression you'd accept the offer that's now on the table? If you have, then unless something significant has changed since that conversation (eg you've been made another (higher) offer for another job) then trying to push for more at this stage looks like you're shifting the goalposts and you're greedy.

ō Talk to your RC and find out whether this client is likely to increase their offer. The RC should have some idea how their client works, and thinks, and may also be aware of any pay ceilings in place at that organisation. They may also have experience and knowledge about potential bonuses and the timeframe before you'll see an increase in your salary anyway.

**SECOND INTERVIEW:**   Again, WOW! Well done you! They like you, and they want you back. Find out from your RC all the same sort of information as you did for the first interview. And again get it in writing:

- Who are you meeting this time?
- Where are you meeting? And when are you meeting?
- What's the likely format of this interview?
- How many other candidates are going to second interview?
- What will be the next stage? Will there be a third round?

Also ask for any feedback from the first interview. Feedback is a particular bonus of working with an RC, generally speaking you don't get such useful feedback when dealing directly with an employer. Typically this is because they don't wish to offend, or they don't want to say something that results in litigation(!), or they simply can't be bothered. When dealing with an RC, clients are more inclined to open up as they have a buffer between themselves and you. Also the client wants to ensure that the RC knows which candidates work for them and why (it saves time, and time is money) for future recruitment needs. So find out from your RC if there were there any areas of concern about you that were expressed by the client. Was there any specific element of your general fabulousness they particularly loved?

The whole thing may simply end up being an exercise in ego massage for you, or it may flag up areas of concern which you'll be able address in the second round of interviews so you can head off and allay any fears they may have. Although if there were any criticisms or concerns that could easily be batted away your RC should have started this process on your behalf. Getting feedback is undoubtedly a worthwhile exercise, so don't let your RC fob you off with some waffle about there not really being any feedback. Of course there may not be, which is frustrating, but do make sure your RC has asked for some. A simple way of doing this would be something along these lines:

You: *That's great news. Did the client offer any feedback?*

RC: *Er, no. No they didn't.*

You: *Oh that's a shame. It'd be so helpful to know of any areas I need to work on, or emphasise... tell you what, would you please ask them for some feedback when you confirm my attendance at the next interview?*

What can the RC say...? They've already stated that the client didn't offer feedback, but they haven't mentioned actively asking for any (which let's face it, they would have done *if* they *had* asked).

♪ Note: if the RC insists they have asked and the client didn't offer any feedback, they may be telling the truth. But you could make a passing comment expressing surprise at the client *actively refusing* to proffer feedback; which if they are fibbing will suggest to them that they have been rumbled without you actually getting into an argy bargy with them. Remember RCs are the same as most people, if you back them into a corner (eg they've fibbed about the refusal to give feedback) you're unlikely to get them to come clean. Wherever possible avoid backing RCs into a corner, not just on this point but on any point. Do your best to give them an exit, a way out, a way to save face without actually having backtrack and admit they've fibbed, exaggerated or manipulated information.

**REJECTION:** Take a deep breath. Don't smash anything (well nothing valuable). And don't cry. (Well you may never have intended to... but personally I can be a softy.) You'll get a lot of well meaning advice from friends later, things along the lines of it not being worth getting upset about, and the client clearly not being worthy of having you working for them. But let's be honest we both know that's poppycock, because if the RC had told you that the client had offered you the job or a second interview you'd have taken it, so clearly you did feel they were worthy of you just seconds ago. However, there are so many reasons for not getting a job that genuinely have nothing to do with you individually that it's vital for your peace of mind for you  to find out why you didn't get the job. Your RC (unless they are unfeeling, or an idiot or both) will hate making the call to tell you that you haven't got the job. Now I know that this isn't really much consolation, but sometimes when you're miserable and suffering there's a vaguely sadistic streak in a lot of us that takes comfort from others suffering too! The RC will usually say something along the lines of *"the client has decided not to take your application any further"* rather than saying something as crass as *"Hey, the client has rejected you"*.

You need to be tough and brave at this point, because you absolutely need to know **why** *the client has decided not to take your application any further*. Obviously you need to know if it's something about your interview technique (then you can work on it). But equally you need to know if you didn't have the right background, or experience, or if the simple truth is that another marginally better candidate pipped you to the post. You may find you have to really push your RC at this stage, because if there *was* negative feedback, their natural inclination will not be to give it to you straight at this point. After all it does rather smack of kicking a man whilst he's down. You need to be cool, calm and collected. Be business-like. Tell the RC you can 'handle the truth' (providing you can keep a straight face and not sound as though you're auditioning for a remake of A Few Good Men). Don't get over emotional, in fact don't get emotional at all. At best a (usually female) RC will feel protective and motherly towards you (putting you in the position of child... not good), at worst you'll come across as weak, fragile, desperate and in need of pity. These are not traits that can possibly work in your favour when handling your RC.

Ironically if the feedback is negative in some ways it's even more important to get it; in case there's something you *can* improve on. Of course the client may have given negative feedback which you elect to ignore, because you feel they're wrong. That's your prerogative of course. But you need to have all the information before you can make the decision to disregard the client's comments.

Remember that there are a host of reasons you may have missed out that aren't down to you. To give you a flavour here are a handful of the most frequently cited reasons given by clients:
  • the post has been filled by an internal candidate (altogether now: AAAAAARGH! GRRRRRRRRRR!).
  • the job has been put on hold (usually due either to lack of

funds, or because they've given up on finding the 'right fit').
• the client has changed the job, so the job spec has changed and they need to restart the search from the beginning.
• the team (or organisation) has been restructured so they are reassessing whether or not they need a new team member.
• they're changing the package (either offering more or less) and are amending their person specification to reflect that.
No matter why you didn't get the job, your RC should be straight on the case giving you some idea of what other jobs are on the horizon, and what their next move on your behalf is going to be.

You may have (indeed should have) told your other RCs about your interview, so you'll need to let them know you didn't get offered the job, and that you're still looking. A word to the wise; total honesty isn't always the best policy. (You may fundamentally disagree with me here, but please bear with me and read on.) I'm not saying you have to lie, but you don't have to be an open book either. If you didn't land the job because of something daft you said or did at the interview (it does happen) or for any other reason that (whether it's fair or not) reflects badly on you, there's no need to tell the other RCs those facts in all their gory detail. It will effect the way they think about you, and remember we want them to envisage the best version of you at all times. So just give them the bare bones: you didn't get the job and your search is still on. Then move straight on to ask if they've got any updates for you or any new jobs to tell you about. Make sure you make those calls. You don't want other RCs relegating you to the bottom of their pile thinking you are, or may be, off the market.

No matter how cross you may be if the client *did* levy an unfair criticism which you feel resulted in you not getting the job, don't vent your anger by ranting or making snide remarks about the client to your RCs. Remember: be professional at all times. It's a surprisingly and unfairly small jump from making one (albeit very funny) sarcastic or caustic remark, to being thought of as a whiny, chippy, resentful, little strop guts who moans all the time.

**SILENCE** (See Troubleshooting Page 110)
There is absolutely no acceptable excuse for silence. If your RC hasn't got a response for you, or at the very least an explanation this is not acceptable. Hassle them, ring them on a daily (or twice daily) basis until you find out what on earth is going on.

# Chapter Sixteen
# THE CLOSE: CONTRACT NEGOTIATION & ACCEPTANCE

You, like me, may often have heard the phrase 'everything is negotiable'. Well, sadly, whilst I don't like to burst anyone's bubble, when it comes to package negotiation that's simply not true (especially in larger organisations). Please understand that I would be thrilled for you to prove me wrong, so do test the water and work with your RC to negotiate a totally unique and deliciously tailored package that meets your every wish. I'm just giving you a heads up that it's unlikely to happen, and to remind you that pigs don't fly.

Typically the lower down you are in an organisation, a general rule of thumb is that you'll have less scope for negotiating your package. But if any part of the package *is* negotiable, it's usually the base salary. Of course some smaller organisations or individual employers may be prepared to negotiate all sorts of elements of the package. This is in part because they have more flexibility, greater autonomy and less fear of setting those dreaded precedents that get rolled out to be whined about in salary negotiations. (I've always thought *"Oooooh but we can't do that, it would set a precedent"* is the illegitimate cousin of *"Oooooh no... it's more than my jobsworth".*) Anyway, your RC should be able to provide guidance on what is or is not going to be negotiable.

♪ Note: if a benefit or package issue is really important to you, do push your RC. One RC recounted a tale of a colleague trying repeatedly to explain to a candidate that the private household who had made him an offer really would not pay for health insurance as part of his package (he'd been used to having it through his previous employer). This RC hadn't spoken to the client, he'd made an (as it turned out, rash) assumption based on past experience with private households. Of course in the end the candidate really pushed the RC, and the RC spoke to the private household who were happy to make arrangements for the candidate to have health insurance. He got his wish. (The RC felt a bit of a berk initially in the office, but with a dollop of spin he managed to convince the candidate, and himself, that it was all down to his outstanding negotiation on the candidate's behalf.)

**YOUR PACKAGE:**

✿ Holiday entitlement: usually (though not always) the contractual holiday entitlement for employees is fixed. So if you're told this is non-negotiable it's unlikely they're playing games, it's just the reality so accept it and move on.

♫ Note: Some organisations have the option of 'buying' extra holiday (ie giving up salary in return for additional days off), it's always worth finding out if this is the case.

The following are elements of a package that are not *usually* negotiable, by which I mean they're either on offer or they're not:

⊘ General Benefits eg free lunch. (You see... there *is* such thing as a free lunch after all...)

⊘ Health Insurance (though remember that as the example on the previous page illustrates, you should judge each situation, it *may* be negotiable in a handful of circumstances).

⊘ Life Insurance: similar situation to Health Insurance.

⊘ Pension, Bonus, Stock Options.

⊘ Gym Membership (Note: big organisations either offer it or don't but smaller ones may have some room for negotiation.)

⊘ Childcare, Car, Interest Free Season Ticket Loan.

⊘ Work mobile phone/blackberry: usually they'll either give you one or they won't, although it can be a matter for discussion in smaller companies. ( ♫  Note: it's not regarded as a great benefit in everyone's eyes; some people feel it just means your boss and colleagues have access to you 24 7.)

**Flexible Benefits**

These are becoming more popular, with organisations increasingly offering flexible benefits packages, or having plans to introduce them. In simple terms, the schemes provide employees with a degree of choice between cash and benefits. They often include the offer of provision of a health plan (eg BUPA), a dental plan, critical illness insurance, childcare, travel insurance, home computers, home/personal mobile phones, and so on and so forth. At its core the idea allows employees to pick and choose which benefits they want, which they then 'purchase' in a salary sacrifice transaction. The cost of the benefits (deducted from salary) are typically less than they'd be if purchasing the benefits outside of the scheme. This isn't solely due to corporate discounts (which on the surface seems the obvious explanation), it's mostly down to the tax and/or NI savings made by taking up the benefits. Of course these benefits are not negotiable, they're either on offer or they're not. But they're *flexible*, as you choose which of the benefits to take, or take the money.

**Negotiation: You or Your RC?** Generally speaking a client will be very clear from the beginning as to whether they wish to negotiate with the RC or with the candidate. In the majority of cases RCs handle the negotiations on your behalf. It would be reassuring I'm sure, if I could tell you that your RC is going to push for as much as possible (being as it means more commission for them). But the reality is that for some RCs their commission structure will be such that by the time it's calculated, an additional £1,000 on your salary may not make a huge difference to their commission (especially if they're way off their monthly or quarterly target anyway). They'll just be happy for you to get the job, so don't kid yourself that the extra commission will definitely be enough of motivator for them. If you're serious that the offer is not good enough then let the RC know that you won't take the job unless the client offers the extra money. But for God's sake only do this if you mean it: now is not the time to play chicken. Do listen to your RC though. They will have knowledge about the clients procedures, and salary ceilings, they will also know if you are likely to receive a hefty bonus (based on recent candidate's experiences) and whether or not you're likely to get salary increase in a few months anyway.

**USEFUL POINTERS:**

🖝 Don't get coy when asking for more money / a better package. Imagine you're negotiating on someone else's behalf if it helps.

🖝 Stick to your guns on points that genuinely matter, but don't be pigheaded over 'points of principle' for the sake of it.

🖝 Double and triple check that your new employer knows of any pre-booked holiday dates.

🖝 Decide on your ideal start date, and push your RC to secure it. You may like a couple of weeks breathing space between jobs if possible (don't forget, in your new role you may well be on the bottom of pile for choosing holidays (newest in a team often is, especially around holiday times such as Christmas)).

🖝 At the end of it all, when you've got a great package and you accept the job, do thank your RC. Despite their faults, and all the handling you've had to do, a thank you means a lot.

# Chapter Seventeen

# TROUBLESHOOTING

Hang on... if you've followed this How to Handle's guidance from the beginning of your relationship with your RC, surely you shouldn't encounter problems that need troubleshooting... should you? No, You shouldn't. However, rather like dogs and children, you can't always predict how an RC is going to react or behave, so it's just possible (highly unlikely, but possible) that you've followed *all* the guidance and they're still playing up. In which case with this chapter we should be able to get them to pull their socks up. Alternatively you may need to troubleshoot because you (shock horror!) *haven't* followed the advice and so you've missed out some key pre-emptive strikes! Well, there's no use in crying over spilt milk; it's true you've made the job harder for yourself... but you've probably already realised that so I won't rub your nose in it. Of course it may be that prior to buying this book you had a relationship with an RC that was in need of tweaking (and that's *why* you got this book). Why ever you're here, you've got (or anticipated) problems with your RC. It's not possible to tackle *all* the potential problems so we're going to troubleshoot the most frequently recurring and significant ones that candidates face.

### #1: My RC keeps calling me about totally inappropriate jobs, what can I do?

If your RC is doing this they either don't remember what it is that you're looking for, or they do and they're ignoring it. Give them the benefit of the doubt. Arrange to speak with them at a time that is mutually convenient, (then obviously do call them at that time). Explain to them that you know they see a lot of candidates so you thought it might be helpful for them if you recapped on your search parameters. After all you know how busy they are and it would be a shame for them to waste their time and yours calling you about job's that aren't of any interest yadda yadda yadda... If they say there's no need and that they know what you are looking for, try to bite your tongue, because as tempting as it may be to say "Well clearly you don't you great buffoon brained orangutan" this will do nothing to help your rapport building. After the conversation email them, thanking them for their time (even if it's through gritted teeth) and, crucially, confirming the key points of your search as discussed.

### #2: My RC appears to have fallen off the end of the earth. He never takes or returns my calls, and never replies to my emails. Help!

Ah, the infamous disappearing RC trick. First get confirmation from the agency that they are in fact still at the agency, and haven't left, gone on hols, been ill, had an accident etc. In fact asking one of their colleagues whether any of those options are applicable may elicit a prompt response. When you call, get whoever you speak to you to give you their name and a time at which they think your RC will be available. Call back at that time.  If the RC still doesn't respond ask to speak to the person you spoke to earlier. Now it's their problem too, so you'll have someone on your RC's back who is actually in the office. When you finally speak, ascertain whether they remember you, your search parameters, and your expectations. Ask them to tell you honestly why they haven't called you, get a verbal commitment from them to stay in touch on a weekly basis; specify a day and time if you so wish, and then email them to confirm this. Warning: Tread carefully, if you badmouth the disappearing RC to his colleagues he may get flak from them, and will regard *you* as the source of that (and not his behaviour). He will not think of you favourably in such circumstances.

### #3: My RC has left the agency. I'd got them perfectly trained, I was handling them like a pro. Now what!?!

That's a real bummer. But it does happen pretty frequently. Find out which RC is taking on the old RC's candidates. Make phone contact and offer to come in to meet with them briefly to outline your job search. They may be hesitant but be persistent and emphasise that you won't take up much of their time. The truth is that you really do need to meet them in order to handle them.

### #4: My RC's a newbie: I don't want to seem mean spirited but can't they practice on somebody else, this is my career we're talking about?!

This is an entirely understandable reaction. No one wants to be the patient with the first leg a doctor sets in plaster, or with the first tooth the dentist drills out. But somebody has to be. Don't let the fact you've got a newbie unsettle you disproportionately, there are of course disadvantages (you'll have worked all of those out already so I'm not going to waste time and print listing them here), but there are a handful of BIG advantages of having a newbie:

• A newbie will have that phenomenal enthusiasm and drive that accompanies arrival in a new job.

• A newbie will be keen to prove just how good they are at their new job (that is prove it to themselves, to their new employers and also (crucially) to you).

• A newbie will have someone supervising them, someone who knows the jobs on the agency's books, is experienced at assessing candidates, and can point out any opportunities or possibilities for you if the newbie have overlooks or misses them (so you're getting two RCs... bargain!)

### #5: I've got an offer through an RC, they've told me not to tell my other RCs, and they're pressuring to me to accept it even though I'm not sure. What do I do?

This is despicable behaviour. They are telling you to keep it under your hat so that no other RC can advise you to wait for a job offer you *are* sure about. But it's playground rules and they're keeping the other kids away from their ball (that's you). Of course you should speak to your other RCs and let them know you have an offer, and find out whether they believe they have any concrete prospects for you at present. (Not just vague possibilities on the horizon). If you're not sure about the offer, think hard to identify what it is that you aren't sure about. Is it the salary, which of course may be negotiable? Or is it the people? Did you feel you wouldn't fit in there? *You* need to make the final decision. Do not allow an RC to bulldoze you into anything you aren't happy with. If needs be remind them that at the end of the day you have no intention of taking a job you would want to leave within a few weeks, which is why you need to be confident it's the right decision. If they have anything between their ears at all, that will remind them that if you leave within 10 weeks (sometimes 3 months (those are the standard periods)) it will result in them either not receiving or having to pay back any commission earned on your placement.

### #6: I've heard tales of RCs asking illegal interview questions. What should I do if it happens to me?

It's up to you. To be clear illegal interview questions are any that could be used to discriminate against you on grounds other than your ability to perform in the role(s) you are interviewing for. So they include questions concerning marital status, sexual preferences, ethnic origin, health status and family plans amongst others. An RC may just foolishly and unintentionally ask such questions (in fairness it is usually done accidentally, due to lack of training). You may feel perfectly comfortable answering such questions anyway, or you may feel it's inappropriate. If you feel it's inappropriate then you could answer in a way that moves around the question. If, for example, you're asked if you're married, you can say something along the lines of "I like to keep my work and personal life separate. Whether or not I'm in a long-term relationship isn't relevant to my future career." Or you may just prefer to point out directly to them that the question they have asked is in fact illegal. The latter is a more blunt approach but if done jovially enough you can do this more easily in interview with an RC than you ever could with a potential employer.

**#7: My RC has acted completely inappropriately, what can I do about it?** That really depends on just how 'inappropriate' the behaviour was, and what outcome you're seeking. You don't want to use a sledgehammer to crack a nut, so you need to assess the severity of the conduct and act accordingly. There are in essence four stages. Bear in mind that anything beyond stage 1, will result in your relationship never being the same with your RC again. But there again, if they warrant stage 3 or 4 (even possibly 2), you're unlikely to want to use them anyway. (1) Contact the RC directly for the remedy you're seeking (which may simply be an apology). (2) Speak informally to their manager. (3) Request a copy of the agency's Complaints Procedure. On receipt of it, write to the person at the agency who is listed as dealing with complaints (or the MD). In your complaint include: the name of the person you're complaining about, the nature of the complaint, the date the incident occurred and, your desired outcome. (4) If you still feel there are unresolved issues then if the agency is a member of a professional body (eg the REC) contact them. The REC has an online complaints form. NOTE: (i) The REC do not accept anonymous complaints (ii) complaints must be made within one year of the event taking place.

**#8: My RC has exceeded my wildest expectations, how can I possibly thank them?** Oh this old chestnut? Happens all the time. Give the RC a humongous thank you and tell everyone (including their Manager/MD, preferably in writing) how totally fabulous that RC is! (Though it's all in the handling of course...).

# Chapter Eighteen

# THE RC HANDLING COMMANDMENTS

☆ Be the Brains of the Operation.

☆ Be knowledgeable but not a know it all.

☆ Be confident but not cocky. Be smart, but not a smart arse.

☆ Be in control, but not bossy.

☆ Be engaging and affable, but not overly matey.

☆ Be strong, but not pigheaded. Be focussed, but not bolshy.

☆ Be open-minded, but not empty-headed and directionless.

☆ Be an eloquent conversationalist, but don't give the impression you have verbal diarrhoea.

☆ Don't be a cold fish, but don't be overly emotional and needy.

☆ Be open to suggestions but don't get bulldozed by an RC with a commission driven glint in their eye.

☆ Don't take personal recommendations at face value.

☆ Don't worry if you don't really like your RC. You don't need to like them, you just have to maintain a professional working relationship (though it'll help if they *think* you like them...).

☆ Be knowledgeable and well informed, that way you can trust your own judgement and decisions.

☆ Don't simply rehash your CV to create your covering letter.

☆ Proof read, proof read, proof read. Do not rely on spell check alone; it won't pick up beauts like 'pubic' when you mean 'public'.

☆ Do not badmouth past or current employers or colleagues, interviewers or other RCs. It's terribly poor form old chap.

☆ Be professional at all times; interviews are not an appropriate forum for discussing the details of your private life.

☆ Make eye contact, shake hands firmly, use names.

☆ Prepare thoroughly, practice religiously and organise with military precision and zeal.

☆ Be the best possible version of yourself in all dealings.

☆ Don't do any of the following (all are genuine examples). Do not turn up for interview: a day late, a week early, hungover, stoned, drunk or in a state of undress. During interview don't: swear constantly, clean your ears, play footsie with the interviewer, burp, launch into an attack on the prime minister of the day, scratch your bottom, fart or pick your nose (and (though one would hope it didn't need saying) do NOT eat it). Post interview do not text clumsily and accidentally text your RC with: lewd suggestions, offers of sexual favours or requests for marijuana. And finally...

☺ SMILE. You see, this RC handling isn't too difficult is it?

# CV CRIB SHEET

♬ NOTE: There have been more books written on writing CVs than you could possibly read in a lifetime. And I'm certainly not going to tackle a topic of that size here, it's not what this book is about. So if you do want to bone up on the CV nitty gritty, pick one of the many books, buy it, read it and apply it. No matter what anyone tells you there is no 'right way' to write a CV, remember that when everyone (including RCs) starts offering advice. Now having said all that here's my tuppence worth...

↳ Don't fanny about with an array of fonts and colours. Keep it simple: one font and one colour.

↳ Length: 2 pages max. (At a push 3.) No one but no one needs their bog standard CV to run to 7+ pages.

↳ Layout: make it clean, sharp, striking and easy to read. Don't use a piddly little font so that you can squeeze all your waffle onto 2 pages without editing the content down. The text will be mean looking, messy and worst of all illegible.

↳ Make use of clear white space: don't have your margins set too narrowly or your sections crunched up too close together.

↳ Allocate space in proportion to the importance of the information you are imparting.

↳ Be consistent in your formatting. By all means use bold, italics and even underlining (if you must). Make use of different font sizes, cases and tabbing. But don't overdo it and be consistent.

↳ Language: use clear, concise, positive, business-like language.

↳ When describing experience and achievements think in terms of features and benefits: I did this... The benefit of which was...

↳ Give a considered, punchy overview of roles, responsibilities and key achievements. Do not reproduce job descriptions and don't drone on and on and on...

↳ Ensure there are no gaps in your chronology.

↳ Tell the truth. Do not exaggerate.

↳ Proof read obsessively. Do not rely on your computer. Check spelling, punctuation, syntax. Then check it again. And again...

↳ Proof read obsessively. Do not rely on your computer. Check spelling, punctuation, syntax. Then check it again. And again...
*(Did you see what I did there? Ensure nothing features twice.)*

↳ And of course once you've crafted your masterpiece remember to actually attach it to the email you're sending to your soon to be handled RC.

*Good luck and good handling!*

# AN A to Z of RECRUITMENT

♫ **NOTE: This is a somewhat eclectic selection of useful tips & terms. Not all of them apply absolutely universally.**

**AGY** ~ Often listed at the end of agency advertisements to flag up that it's an agency ad.

**Applicant** ~ You BC (Before Consultant). As far as an agency is concerned you're an applicant until you're actually on their books and registered as a candidate.

**Client** ~ Most emphatically not you. The RC's client is your potential employer; and that's who pays the price of recruiting you. (In all its possible interpretations).

**Candidate** ~ That's you *after* you've registered with an RC.

**CV** ~ Curriculum Vitae. You know what it is so I won't insult you by explaining it, but included because there's a point that needs emphasising. If you insist in writing it out in full whether in a covering letter or email, or on the CV itself, for God's sake do spell it correctly. It's astonishing how often those two words get misspelt. (Literal translation from Latin 'course of life'.)

**CV Search** ~ Generally used to describe the activity undertaken by RCs where they search jobsites' databases for candidates. Candidates usually register CVs for free, whilst agencies pay a fee for access to the database. Typically RCs search by experience, salary requirements, skills, qualifications, location & keywords.

**Experience Required** ~ Has always seemed pretty self explanatory to me, but I can only assume it isn't looking at some applications received. The phrase is not usually included in an advert just for the heck of it; it means that you need experience. So if you insist on applying for jobs requiring relevant experience and you have none, don't be surprised if you damage your credibility with your prospective RC.

**FMCG** ~ (abbr) Fast Moving Consumer Goods, also sometimes known as Consumer Packaged Goods (CPG). It's used in job adverts when an agency doesn't want to identify the specific company they're recruiting for, but clearly needs to indicate the industry. FMCG companies produce products that sell quickly, and in large volumes, at relatively low cost. Examples: toiletries, cosmetics, plastic goods, some food products, stationery. Well known FMCG companies include: Nestle, Kraft Jacobs Suchard, Procter and Gamble, Unilever, Coca-Cola, PepsiCo & Kleenex.

**Holding Pattern** ~ Conventionally used to describe planes circling an airport waiting to land. *Candidate in a holding pattern:* a common technique adopted by RCs wishing to hold onto good candidates even if the agency hasn't got many (or sometimes any) appropriate jobs on their books (or even on the horizon) ie metaphorically *you're* the plane. *Client in a holding pattern:* a technique used on clients to the advantage of a candidate; for example when an RC stalls a client (ie now *they're* the plane) if a candidate can't decide whether or not to accept a job. In some cases it's best for the client not to know this (...it irritates certain clients to think that the candidate isn't completely cock a hoop and cart wheeling in ecstasy and gratitude at the thought of working for them).

**Internal Candidate** ~ the bane of RC's lives. These are the individuals who already work at an organisation and land the jobs for which an RC has bust their buns sourcing prospective candidates. In especially frustrating cases the client only uses an RC so the process can be seen to be fair whilst intending to recruit internally anyway (which of course has the bonus of being cheaper). You'll rarely get a client to admit any of this.

**Job Description** ~ This is one of the documents the client usually provides for RCs, and it essentially covers the basics of the job and what will be expected of the successful candidate. Details covered include: job title, location, the organisation, the team, the role itself and what it entails (duties and responsibilities), how the role will develop, working conditions, salary and benefits package.

**Job Spec** ~ (abbr) Job Specification. Another document usually supplied by the client for the RC. Essentially it outlines the profile of the ideal person for the job; often split into 'essential' and 'desirable' qualities. Sometimes called: Person Specification.

**MS Office Skills Tests** ~ Some agencies run these tests as standard (Note: not only for support roles). If they run the tests at all they will nearly always test your skills with Microsoft Word. Excel and PowerPoint are also frequently tested and occasionally Access. Typing speed tests are often run as standard too.

**Numeracy Tests** ~ Sometimes used by RCs and/or employers to test your basic mathematical ability.

**OTE** ~ Opportunity To Earn. Usually used in advertisements for some sort of sales based job, and used to entice debt ridden grads (amongst others) with an often unrealistic (or at best a somewhat optimistic projection of) potential salary.

**PA** ~ (abbr) Salary on a per annum basis ie per year. Also short for Personal Assistant. (Unlikely to refer to a Personal Address system in a job ad... though I suppose it could... at a stretch).

**Person Specification** ~ See Job Specification.

**Placement** ~ How RCs describe placing you in a job. ie When you land a job through an RC, that's a placement for them.

**PW** ~ (abbr) Salary on a per week basis, used for temp jobs.

**Pro Rata** ~ Latin, meaning in proportion, according to a factor that can be calculated exactly. So if you see £28,000 Pro Rata advertised for a three day a week job you'll actually probably be earning approximately £16,800 pa. It's used for part time roles.

**Psychometric Tests** ~ Sometimes carried out by RCs and sometimes by employers (and sometimes by neither). 3 main types: ability, personality and interest (Note: both personality and interest tests are more like psychometric questionnaires). Tests may be administered by pencil and paper or by computer. They may be taken at RC's offices, at interviews with potential employers, at assessment centres or online. A particular score is often set, which you need to achieve in order to proceed.

**Quote Ref** ~ If an advert asks you to quote the reference given (sometimes a number, sometimes a code, sometimes a name) then make sure you do so, or the RC may not have a clue which job you've applied for (especially if your covering email or letter hasn't made it clear... which of course it should have done.).

**Remuneration** ~ Big word for how much you get paid, and one that is often misspelt or mispronounced. Don't fall into that trap. I wish I had a pound for every candidate who told me they'd like a job where 'their effort would be reflected in their renumeration' (for the less eagle eyed, the 'n' and 'm' have been transposed).

**Zip Code** ~ American postcodes. If a UK candidate puts 'zip code' on their CV it suggests they've used a template and are either too lazy to change it, or too stupid to know how to do so; neither is good. Use 'postcode'.

**Zodiac** ~ Do not include your star sign on your CV. Nor should you include a list of favourite magazines, TV Soaps or anything in a similar vein. It's irrelevant, and frankly its a tad weird.

# Index

Order online at
www.shortstackpublishing.com

Forthcoming Short Stack Titles

How to Handle Christmas
How to Handle Your Wedding
How to Handle Burns Night
How to Handle Naming Your Dog
How to Handle Being a Newlywed
How to Handle Rejection
How to Handle a Mid Life Crisis
How to Handle Having No
Discernible Talent
How to Handle Drinking, Dining,
Dozing and Dreaming with Your Dog